SUPER
Pop-up Reports
for

AMERICAN HISTORY

By Susan Kapuscinski Gaylord

SCHOLASTIC
PROFESSIONAL BOOKS

New York • Toronto • London • Auckland • Sydney
Mexico City • New Delhi • Hong Kong

DEDICATION

for my son, Brendan—my assistant, my idea man, and my friend

Cover design by Pam Simmons

Interior design by Melinda Belter

Interior illustrations by Susan Kapuscinski Gaylord

Pop-up reports created by Diana Saville (page 5); Allison Soupcoff (page 8); Katherine Vetne (page 25); and Joey Pelletier (page 40)

ISBN 0-590-58101-5

Copyright © 2000 by Susan Kapuscinski Gaylord

Printed in the U.S.A.

Contents

Acknowledgments

Though I have been teaching how to make pop-up reports to students since 1996, the book originated back in 1990. I had received a grant from the Lowell Historic Preservation Commission, U.S. Department of the Interior, to do the Lowell Multicultural Book Project in Lowell, Massachusetts. I spent two months working with adults who represented different ethnic groups in the city and who each made and then exhibited a book about his or her family history. I owe the form of what would become pop-up reports to Regina Fuller, who brought in an old children's book to use as a model for her book. The book opened up into four rooms and the walls of each rooms featured pop-up elements. Regina's book was packed with information about her Polish family and included pictures of Ellis Island, her church, and her family.

In 1996, my son's fifth-grade was doing a unit on family heritage, and I proposed working on a book with them. When I reviewed the slides of the books from the Lowell Multicultural Book Project, I decided that Regina's book would be the most interesting for students to make. Each student created a four-room report about his family heritage. The project was a great success with the students, the teachers, and the parents. I am grateful to Pat Beckwith, Tony Lee, Claudia Peresman, and the Alpha team of fifth graders at the Rupert A. Nock Middle School in Newburyport, Massachusetts.

Over the past two years, I have taught this structure to many groups of teachers and students and modified the process along the way, incorporating both suggestions from others and the results of my own observations. I thank all my students, young and old, who always teach me as I teach them.

The project became **Super Pop-up Reports for American History** when I approached Scholastic Professional Books and began working with editor Virginia Dooley. Starting from the immigration aspect of family heritage, she expanded the focus to eight topics in American history. It has been a pleasure to combine my love of history with my love for teaching and making things.

While I was writing this book, I returned to the Nock Middle School in Newburyport for a final test run. Thanks again to Pat Beckwith, and to the 1998 team of fifth graders who made books about Colonial America. I appreciate their suggestions and comments and the eagerness with which they worked.

In the Suggested Readings sections, I was helped by Eloise Schoeppner at the Newburyport Public Library Children's Room; Christina Davis and Ellen Menesale at the Nock Middle School Library, Beverly Bittarelli of Book Ends in Winchester, Massachusetts; Gwen Holt from the Banbury Cross Children's Bookshop in Hamilton, Massachusetts; and Jean Berry. They helped me narrow the choices and sent me home with stacks of books.

Last but not least, I thank my family, Charlie, Brendan, and Kendra who are with me all the way. They give me encouragement when I need it, advice whether I want it or not, and love, always.

4

Introduction

I've made pop-up reports with more than a thousand students over the past four years, and they've been a hit with kids, teachers, and parents. Kids like them because they are fun to work on and look great when completed. Teachers like them because they motivate their students to do research and make great display pieces for parents' night and other school functions. Parents like them because they are impressive, dramatic, and—unlike the dioramas and posters we beg our children to part with—they fold up and can be stored easily.

At the start of my workshops, I hold up what looks like a flat book and tell students, "This is what we're going to make." The students are all looking but not particularly enthused. When I open the book and they see the structure unfold, their eyes pop and their jaws drop. "Wow! We're going to make that?" they ask.

When creating pop-up reports with students, I always build the structure first. I refer to it as a building that has four rooms and tell them that each room has two walls and a floor. I find students are more motivated in their research and writing when they have a structure waiting to be filled. They know where their efforts are going and are excited by the prospect. Although it may not be history, students are also learning as they construct their buildings. They have to listen and follow directions, use fine motor skills, and develop visual-spatial skills and problem-solving abilities.

I also like the way the pop-up reports involve students of various abilities. Constructing the buildings allows students with kinesthetic and spatial intelligence to shine. An eighth-grade boy who was way ahead of the rest of the class in math found making the building to be extremely challenging. Several seats away, a student who usually had a tough time keeping up in class was a whiz. When it's time to fill in the report, students with artistic ability and a good design sense, and those with strong research and writing skills, can show their strengths.

As students make these pop-up reports, you'll find a wide range of results. Some kids will work incredibly carefully as they make their building. Everything will be folded and glued precisely. Other kids will take a more freewheeling approach. There will be crooked folds and gaps where two pieces were attached. It really doesn't matter. When they are full of illustrations and material, they will all look good, each in its own way.

Super Pop-up Reports for American History is presented in two sections. The first part shows how to construct the building and make the pop-ups. The second part has specific material and templates for eight topics in American history: Native Americans, Explorers, Colonial America, the Revolutionary War, the Underground Railroad, Pioneers, the Civil War, and Immigration.

The step-by-step instructions for constructing the building are divided into four parts. In the introduction to each part, I describe the basic principles and give suggestions for working with the class. The directions themselves are written as if I were talking directly to the students. You may certainly modify the steps, but I can guarantee that if you follow them exactly, you will be successful.

The next section features a reproducible Report Planner to help students plan their research and their report. Students can use it to map out their rooms and plan for writing and illustrations. It is helpful for students to have a folder to hold their Report Planner and the material they collect.

The fun part is putting it all together. All the writing and illustrations are done on separate sheets of paper and glued in. This collage approach is easier than writing and drawing directly on the pages. Text and illustrations can be glued directly to the walls and floor or pop up and out. In the directions for adding text and illustrations, I begin with the simplest methods, moving on to more advanced techniques. Students can go as far as they are comfortable. The report will look great even if a student includes just a few simple text boxes and illustrations. Students who easily grasp the pop-up construction can help other students.

Fourth- and fifth-grade teachers I worked with had their students do their research outside of class, but all the material was kept in the classroom and the building was filled during class time. Older students usually did it as a homework project, but some class time was allotted for help with the pop-ups.

In Part 4, I have included directions and patterns for a teaching sample for you to make. It will serve as a learning tool for you and as a reference for students as they work on their reports. I suggest that you begin by making at least one sample on your own before teaching the class.

In Part 5, there is specific information for the eight American history topic areas. Each section contains suggested topics for the reports, a few resources that I found particularly helpful, and suggested readings—two fiction titles whose subject is in that period of history. Templates follow. They are intended as a supplement. Students should be encouraged to make their own drawings if they can, and to look for other sources of imagery. The book concludes with general patterns for writing templates and banners.

Here are my suggestions and strategies for helping your students create pop-up reports.

Before Getting Started

1. Make a teaching sample. Follow the directions on pages 8-20 to construct the building. Then follow the directions on pages 40-48 to fill the teaching sample with pop-ups, banners, and more.

2. Gather the materials you'll need to create another teaching sample to demonstrate the process to the class.

With the Class

1. Introduce the project and the research topics to the class. Show students the teaching sample.

2. Build the buildings with the class. Allow at least 90 minutes.

3. Hand out copies of the Report Planner and begin the project. See that each student has a folder to hold all the material gathered during the course of the project.

4. Use the building you previously made to demonstrate how to fill in the building. This should take about 45 minutes. Keep the teaching samples in the classroom for students to refer to as they work.

5. Allow some class time for questions and troubleshooting and/or actual work on the books.

These reports are an adventure for the entire class. Gather the materials, make your own sample, inspire your class, and have fun!

Making the Building

1

What I really like about these projects is that they are easier to make than they look. How many things in life can we say that about? I prefer to work with a class of 20 to 25, but I have often made them with groups as large as 50, with the help of three assistants. The secret is giving the group precise directions and working together. I do not let anyone work ahead of the group; I lose time and the ability to keep an eye on the group when I am undoing mistakes students have made.

I will use the metaphor of constructing a building with four rooms throughout this section. The process is divided into four steps: 1) making the rooms, 2) marking the rooms, 3) attaching the rooms to each other, and 4) attaching the covers. When I teach, I demonstrate each of the steps and then have students do them. I don't go on to the next step until everyone is finished.

I allow one and a half hours to complete the project. I have also divided the construction into two 45-minute periods. In the first session, we make the individual rooms; in the second, we mark them, attach them to each other, and add the covers. To accomplish the project in these time periods, students must work quickly and steadily. You might want to plan for more time, especially the first time you do it.

GETTING STARTED

Materials

Each student will need:

4 sheets of 8 1/2-by-14-inch paper (legal size) for the walls

4 sheets of 7-by-7-inch paper for the floors

2 sheets of 7 3/4-by-7 1/4-inch posterboard or oaktag for the cover

1 piece of 36-inch ribbon for the closure

Tools

Each student will need:

ruler (I use standard wooden rulers. The rulers should be about 1-inch wide.)

scissors

pencil

glue stick

scrap paper for gluing (I use old phone-book or catalog pages.)

Variations

I use legal size paper because it is a standard size and makes a comfortable size book to work with. You can change the size of the paper (and the size of the book) if you follow these rules:

1. The paper for the floor must be a square.

2. The length of the paper for the walls must be twice the width of the square.

3. The width of the paper for the wall determines the height of the room. The height of the room can vary.

4. The cover should always be larger than the finished sections. I added 1/4-inch to the height and the width. The thicker the paper you use for the sections, the more allowance you should add.

Choosing Paper

I chose the 8 1/2-by-14-inch size because it is readily available as legal-size copy paper. I have used standard 20-pound copy paper. I have also purchased 60-pound text paper from a local printer. The heavier paper is nice but not necessary. In most of my workshops, I use heavier stock for the covers including posterboard, oaktag, or any other heavy paper or light cardboard. I save time by having all the paper cut to size by the printer. You might try asking a local printer for donations. Allow extra paper; there will probably be mistakes. I use 1/8- to 1/4-inch ribbon, which I buy in 10-yard rolls, for the ties.

Tips and Tactics for Gluing

Glue is what holds the building together. Both the kind of glue you use and the way you put it on makes a difference. Even though students are sure they know how to glue—they've been doing it since at least kindergarten, haven't they?—I make them do it my way.

My preference is to use glue sticks—there is no easier or safer way to glue. My favorite brand of glue stick is UHU by Faber-Castell because it allows you to lift and reposition things before the glue dries. However, you need to make sure you apply firm pressure after you've glued. I also like to use colored glue stick—which goes on purple but dries clear because the students can see exactly where the glue is. Other glue sticks are tackier and make a firmer bond; therefore they stick more easily but are harder to maneuver. Experiment to see what works best for you.

Here's my trick: When you are gluing two pieces of paper together, only put glue on one piece. If the pieces are different sizes, the glue goes on the smaller piece.

I also give my students the following gluing tips when we make our buildings:

1. Don't roll the glue sticks up too high. It only needs to be about 1/8-inch above the container.

2. Don't press too hard. If you get globs of glue on your paper, it means you are pressing too hard.

3. Hold the glue stick perpendicular to the surface of the paper to get the broadest stroke of glue.

4. Always place a larger piece of scrap paper under the paper you are gluing. This is because you want to get glue on the edges of the paper and scrap paper will protect the table from glue.

5. To glue, start in the center at one edge and go up the paper and over the top edge onto the scrap paper. Continue applying the glue in stripes from the center up. After the top half of the paper is covered, reverse direction and apply in stripes going down the paper.

6. Work steadily so that the glue doesn't dry before you attach the pieces.

7. After the entire surface is covered with glue, remove the scrap paper and fold it in half with the glue on the inside. If you leave paper with glue on your workspace, you'll end up getting glue where you don't want it.

8. After attaching the pieces, apply firm pressure by smoothing the paper with your thumb or your hand. Do it to both sides that have been glued.

STEP 1
MAKING THE ROOMS

I begin by explaining the basic principles to students: We are using one 8 1/2-by-14-inch sheet of paper and one 7-by-7-inch sheet of paper for each room—the long sheet of paper forms the walls, and the square makes the floor. I make the first two rooms step-by-step together with the students. The first time I give all the directions. The second time I ask them to tell me what the next step is. Then I have them complete the last two rooms on their own. I stop and tell them to ask me if they are unsure at any step. And I remind them to work carefully. It's not a race and they can't go on to the next step until everyone is finished. Some kids get it right away, others take a little longer, but they usually all understand by the time they've made all four. I always complete one room at a time, rather than work in assembly-line style to help students better comprehend the process.

Making the Walls

1. Start with one sheet of the 81/2-by-14-inch paper. Fold it in half the short way.

2. Hold the folded paper in front of you so that the fold is on the left.

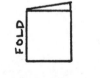

Making the Tabs

1. Lay the ruler on top of the paper so that the bottom of the ruler is even with the bottom of the paper.

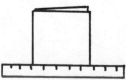

2. With one hand on each side, place your thumbs firmly on the ruler and your fingers under the paper. Bend the top of the page forward and make a fold along the edge of the ruler.

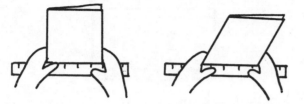

3. Remove the ruler and go over the fold to make a smooth crease. You can use the side of the ruler to gently flatten the crease even more. Be careful: If you apply too much pressure, the paper might rip. Unfold the tab.

4. Take the lower left corner of the tab and fold it on the diagonal to meet the crease, making a small triangle.

5. Unfold the triangle and cut off the corner along the fold line. You will be cutting through two layers of paper.

6. Open the paper and recrease both tabs so that they are facing in.

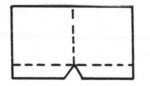

Attaching the Floor to the Tabs

1. Apply glue to the top of the left tab. (See Tips and Tactics for Gluing on page 10) **Remember: You want a thin coat covering the entire tab.**

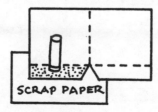

SCRAP PAPER

2. Place the square sheet of paper (the floor) on top of the left wall. Line up the bottom of the square with the tab fold. Notice that the floor does not completely cover the wall.

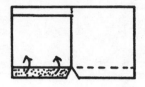

3. Fold the tab up and press to adhere to the floor. Remember that all that is holding the book together is glue. Pressure is important.

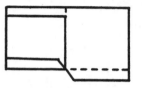

4. Take the top right corner of the floor (it's on the inside, at the fold) and fold it on the diagonal to meet the bottom left corner to form a triangle.

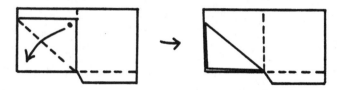

5. Unfold the square.

6. Apply glue to the top of the right tab.

7. Stand up the two walls. Adjust the two walls so that the floor covers the right tab. Press the floor to the right tab to adhere.

8. Your first room is complete! Fold it flat again and run your thumb or the edge of the ruler along the folds to make them as smooth as possible. Set the first room aside and make three more.

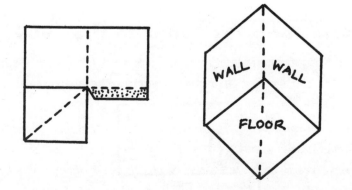

STEP 2
MARKING THE ROOMS

I added this step when I found that students were gluing sections together incorrectly—so that some rooms had floors and others had ceilings. Since I started having them mark the top right corner of each section before gluing, my success rate has gone up to almost 100 percent.

1. Place the folded room in front of you so that the fold is on the left and the floor is on the bottom. To check if it's in the right position, pull the right corner back. You should see the point of the floor triangle inside.

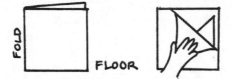

2. If it is correct, use a pencil and lightly make an X on the right corner of the closed room.

3. Mark the other three rooms using the same technique.

Tip

Before going on to the next step, check each student's work to make sure the X's are in the correct place. An alternative is to have students check each other's work.

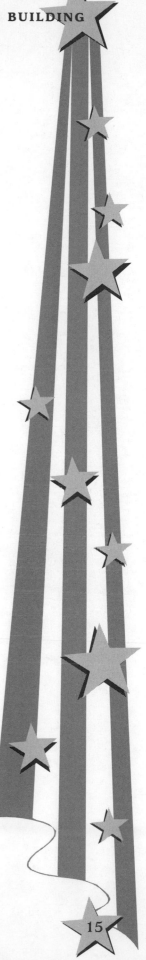

STEP 3
ATTACHING THE ROOMS
TO EACH OTHER

Once the rooms are complete, the next step is to glue the rooms to each other. The rooms are glued together in a stack. The front wall of one room is glued to the back wall of the next. When the process is completed, there is a flat stack of four rooms. When the students are finished gluing the rooms together, I have them open up the buildings. This is always an exciting moment. However, I don't let them keep them open, because there are always a few who want to glue those last rooms together so that they will never close again. If they're all open, I can't tell which ones have been glued and which ones haven't.

1. Place one room flat on the table so that the X is in the upper right-hand corner. Cover the entire surface with glue.

2. Place the second room on top of the first room. The X on the second room should be facing you in the upper right corner again. It can be a little tricky to line up the rooms. I find it easiest to line up the side folds first. Lift the top wall and smooth the bottom wall to help the glue adhere.

3. Continue with the next two rooms. Apply glue to the top room and then place the next room on top. Make sure the X is always in the top right corner.

4. You are finished when you have a stack of four rooms. ***Do not put glue on the top room.***

5. Open your construction. It will look like a building with four rooms.

STEP 4
ATTACHING THE COVERS

The last step in constructing the building is attaching the covers and the ribbon closure. The covers are attached one side at a time. The sheets of paper used for the cover are a little larger than the rooms. The covers will be flush with the rooms at the side folds and along the floor. They will stick out a little beyond the rooms on the top and the open side.

Attaching the Top Cover

1. Place the book in front of you so that the fold is on the left and the X is in the upper right corner. Draw a light pencil line across the middle. This is to remind you where the ribbon goes.

2. Cover the entire surface of the top room with glue.

3. Fold the ribbon in half. Place half of the ribbon along the pencil line. The ribbon will stick to the glue. Place the other half behind the rooms. The ends of the ribbon should be even, so that you can tie a bow later to keep the book closed.

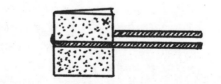

4. Notice that the cover is a rectangle. You will be using it so that it is taller than it is wide. Place the cover on top of the rooms so that it is even with the left side (where the side folds are) and even with the floor. *It is very important to have the cover flush with the left side of the building. If the cover extends beyond the left side, the building will not open all the way.*

5. Flip the building over so that the fold is on the right. A portion of the cover should show on the top and left side of the book.

6. To help the glue adhere, pull back all the rooms and smooth the wall that has been attached to the cover.

Attaching the Bottom Cover

1. Flip the book over so that the fold is on the right. Draw a light pencil line across the middle of the paper to serve as a reminder for the ribbon.

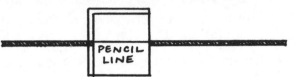

PENCIL LINE

2. Cover the paper completely with glue.

3. Place the ribbon across the middle of the book.

4. Align the back cover with the top of the front cover and then attach the back cover to the back of the book. Check that the cover is flush with the fold on the right side.

5. Open and press on the wall that was just attached to the cover to help it adhere.

6. Congratulations! You've built the building. Put your name on your book. If you don't want it to show, write it on the underside of the floor of the first room.

Tip
You can help the glue adhere by pressing the finished building overnight. Wrap the book in waxed paper and place it under a stack of heavy books. This is a helpful but not essential step.

COMMON PROBLEMS AND SOLUTIONS

- **The student folds the triangle on the tab at the open edge instead of at the fold.**

When she cuts the triangle, it is at the edges instead of in the middle and the tab has not been divided in two. This is not a problem. Just fold and cut a triangle at the folded side and proceed.

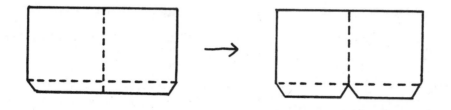

- **The student glues a floor to each tab.**

If you catch the mistake before the glue is completely dry, you may be able to pull one floor piece off. I try to emphasize the fact that we are using one sheet of paper for the wall and one sheet of paper for the floor, but it doesn't always work. One way to head off the problem is to pass out paper for one room at a time.

FLOOR   FLOOR

- **The student puts glue on the bottom of the tab instead of the top and glues the floor under the tab.**

In this case, it's usually best to start over. Even if you you can pull the floor off, the glue on the underside of the tab will remain sticky.

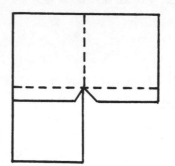

- **The student forgets to make the diagonal fold in the floor.**

This is easy to fix. Fold up the section and press it together to make the crease in the floor

- **The student opens his building and discovers that there are both floors and ceilings.**

Try to gently pry the problem rooms apart. If this doesn't work, he'll have to start over.

- **The rooms start to separate from each other as the student works on the contents.**

There is a fair amount of stress on the structure as it opens and closes. The problem area is usually along the side folds, especially at the bottom. I use Elmer's glue for repair. I put a small amount of glue on a piece of scrap paper and slip the scrap paper between the separating rooms to apply the glue. I squeeze the rooms together and wipe off any glue that has oozed out. Then I press the book under heavy books or other weights until the glue dries.

Planning the Report

2

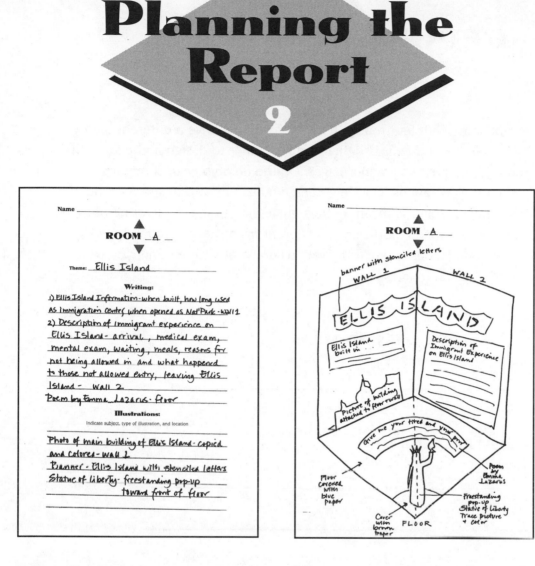

Name _____

▲
ROOM __A__
▼

Theme: Ellis Island

Writing:

1) Ellis Island Information- when built, how long used as Immigration Center, when opened as Nat'l Park - W2/12
2) Description of Immigrant experience on Ellis Island - arrival, medical exam, mental exam, waiting, meals, reasons for not being allowed in and what happened to those not allowed entry, leaving Ellis Island - Wall 2.
Poem by Emma Lazarus - floor

Illustrations:
Indicate subject, type of illustration, and location

Photo of main building of Ellis Island - copied and colored - Wall 1
Banner - Ellis Island with stenciled letters
Statue of Liberty - freestanding pop-up
                  toward front of floor

Name _____

▲
ROOM __A__
▼

banner with stenciled letters
WALL 1   WALL 2

ELLIS ISLAND

Ellis Island built in

Description of Immigrant Experience on Ellis Island

Picture of building attached to floor - wall

Give me your tired and your poor

Floor covered with blue paper

Poem by Emma Lazarus

Freestanding pop-up Statue of Liberty Trace picture + color

Cover with brown paper

FLOOR

Planning the report is an ongoing process. As students complete their research, they can begin to plan how they will display the information and the types of images and illustrations they will use. On the following pages, you'll find a reproducible Report Planner. For each room, there are two pages: one to summarize the writing and list the illustrations and the other to fill in a floor plan of where things go. Above is an example of a completed plan for one room.

Encourage students to collect as many illustrations and as much material as they can before they map out their rooms. This will allow them to select what works best to tell their story. The Report Planner is meant to be a guide, not a precise plan that must be followed exactly. Students will think of new ideas as they work and should try them out. Just as they edit the various drafts of their writing, they will edit their assembly of text and images.

▲

REPORT PLANNER

▼

Your report is a building with four rooms. Each room should have a different theme and include both illustrations and text. Use this Report Planner to design and plan each room. For each room, there are two planner pages. On the first, you can summarize the text and describe the illustrations. On the second, you can draw a diagram of the room's layout. The Report Planner is meant to be a guide, not a precise plan that must be followed exactly. Your finished report may be different from the one you mapped out in your Report Planner. Just as you edit the various drafts of your writing, you can edit your assembly of text and images.

My topic is

_____.

My four themes (one per room) are:

Theme 1. _____

Theme 2. _____

Theme 3. _____

Theme 4. _____

My report is due on: _____.

Name _____

▲
ROOM _____
▼

Theme: _____

Writing:

_____

_____

_____

_____

_____

_____

_____

Illustrations:

Indicate subject, type of illustration, and location

_____

_____

_____

_____

Name _____

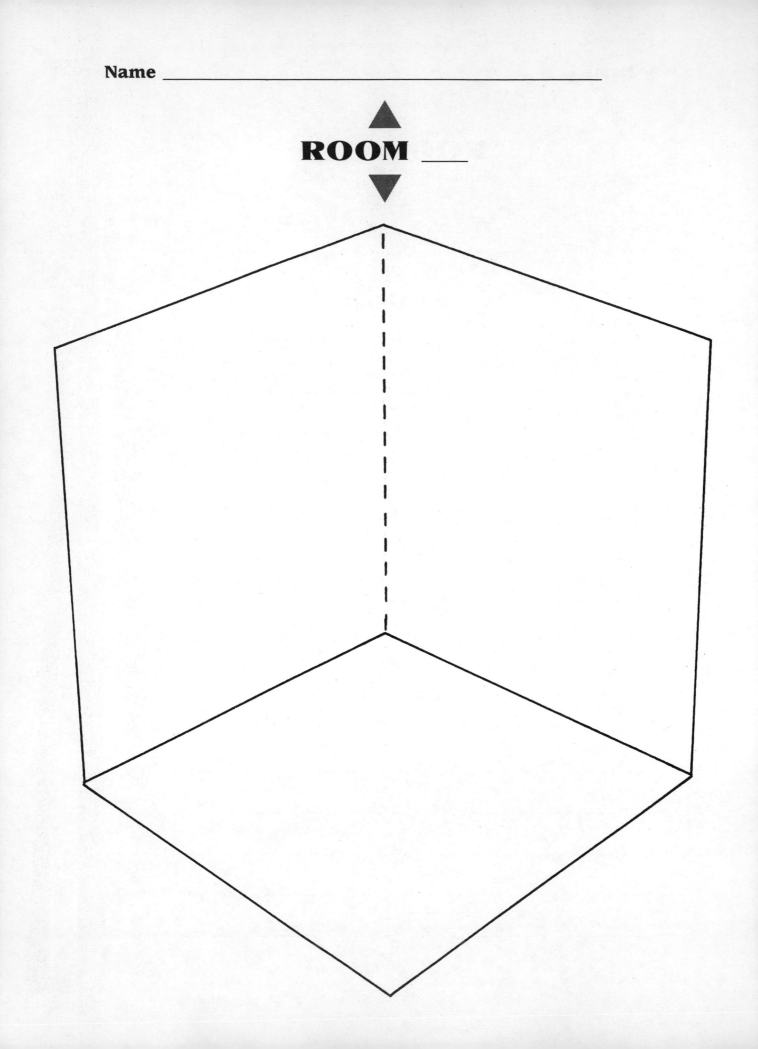

ROOM ___

Creating the Report

3

Now the fun starts! It's time for students to fill their buildings with the results of their research. In this section, you'll find writing suggestions and tips for creating the illustrations, as well as directions for how to place the elements in the building. You'll also find step-by-step directions for creating two-dimensional and three-dimensional elements.

Before working with the students, I suggest making a teaching sample using the patterns on pages 40-48. This will give you a chance to learn the techniques and have a sample to show students.

Both elements, text and illustrations, are done on separate sheets of paper and then glued into the book.

▲ GETTING STARTED ▼

Materials and Tools

Each student will need:

scissors

glue stick and scrap paper

markers, black and colored

colored pencils

index cards or heavier stock paper for pop-up

colored papers to use for backgrounds and mounting. Collect construction paper, wrapping paper, brown grocery bags, wallpaper samples, thin pieces of cloth, etc.

tape

Optional

Items to have available for the class:

rubber stamps—letters, numbers, patterns; stamps on rollers for a continuous band of a shape

stamp pads

scissors that cut shaped edges—zigzags, scallops, deckles, etc.

stencils for letters and patterns

picture corners—used in old-fashioned photo albums, these can still be purchased in some photo and stationery stones. Use them to attach illustrations.

access to a photocopier

▲
PLANNING THE TEXT
▼

Each room in the building will include sections of text. The text can be handwritten or typed. For handwritten text, use the writing templates on pages 91–93. These templates can be copied and written on. Another option is to place the template behind a sheet of paper and use the lines as guidelines. When writing by hand, mistakes can be a problem. Mistakes can be avoided by writing a draft in pencil then going over the writing with marker or pen. Be careful about using correction fluid. Test it first, as the ink will sometimes bleed or it will be difficult to write over the correction fluid.

Creating the text on a computer makes it easier to revise and correct. If the writing is done on the computer, I suggest picking an easy-to-read font for the main sections of text. I also think it's best to pick one style for the main text of each room, if not all four. Titles and headlines can be larger, bolder, and more decorative. Experiment with printing on colored paper.

HARD TO READ

ELLIS ISLAND
ELLIS ISLAND WAS THE FIRST STOP FOR MANY IMMIGRANTS AS THEY ARRIVED IN AMERICA.

ELLIS ISLAND
Ellis Island was the first stop for many immigrants as they arrived in America.

EASY TO READ

The text can be presented and displayed in many creative ways. All of the text can be on one sheet of paper, which can be mounted on a wall or a floor, or the text can be cut up and mounted in smaller sections. The sections of text do not have to be rectangles—they can be squares, circles, even triangles. Lines of writing can be curved or written in different colors. Use stencils or rubber stamps or a different color for a title or to highlight a piece of information.

PLANNING THE ILLUSTRATIONS

Here are just a few ways to collect and create illustrations for reports.

1. Draw illustrations using the images that have been collected as reference.

2. Try cut paper or collage techniques. Instead of drawing images, build them from pieces of colored paper. This gives a bold, graphic look.

3. Photocopy images on a copier. For an interesting effect, use colored pencils to add color to black and white photocopies. Not all images copy well. Some may be too dark; some may not have enough contrast. Experiment with the light and dark settings on the copier to get the best results. Making color copies is another option—though they are expensive.

4. Trace maps, drawings, or photographs. If the illustration is dark enough, use regular white paper to trace it. If not, place tracing paper over the image and trace it. Here's a tracing tip: After tracing an image, turn the tracing paper over and go over the lines with a pencil. Turn the tracing paper right side up, place it on another piece of paper, and draw over the lines. The pencil from the back of the tracing paper will be transferred to the new paper. Go over the lines with pencil or marker.

5. Download pictures from the Internet.

6. Cut out pictures from magazines and catalogs.

7. Scan images into the computer and then print them out

8. Use the templates provided in Part 5 (page 49). The templates can be colored or adapted and personalized any way you choose.

ADDING TWO-DIMENSIONAL ELEMENTS

Setting Up the Room

Each of the elements added to each room is created on a separate sheet of paper and then glued into the building. As in constructing the building, the gluing technique is important. (See Tips and Tactics for Gluing on page 10)

I prefer to tack on all the materials for a whole room, evaluate it, and then do the final gluing. I use pieces of tape folded into thirds. Even though the arrangement has been mapped out in the Report Planner, you might find that moving something up an inch or over a half an inch makes a big difference in the final look.

Mounting Text and Illustrations

Create a frame for a section of text or an illustration by mounting it on a larger sheet of paper. Construction paper, wrapping paper with interesting patterns or stripes, wallpaper samples, and pieces of thin cloth all can be used to mount illustrations. They also can be used to cover an entire wall or floor. The paper can correspond to the subject of the report. If the report is about immigration, the background might feature the colors of an immigrant's home flag. Dark greens and browns would be appropriate for the northern explorers, while a bright Caribbean blue might be more suggestive for Columbus. A piece of brown grocery bag that has been torn rather than cut might suggest the buffalo hides that were so important to the Plains Indians.

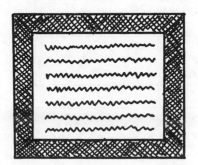

Creating Borders

Borders are a good way to add pattern and color to each room. Borders can frame an illustration or a section of text or outline the entire wall or floor. The borders should relate to the topic or time period of the report. For example, I used traditional clothing and craft designs for the Native American borders and used wallpaper border patterns as inspiration for the Colonial American borders.

Here is an easy way to design borders that has been successful for me and for students. Rather than come up with an entire design all at once, I build the border line by line. It is best to experiment on scrap paper until you come up with a design you like.

Another way to design a border is to draw a zigzag line in the border. Fill in the spaces up and below the line with different shapes.

I sometimes mark off the corners into squares and put a small drawing or symbol in each corner. I then make a border design on the four sides.

Tip

Use rubber stamps to make a simple border pattern.

ADDING THREE-DIMENSIONAL ELEMENTS

Three-dimensional elements, such as pop-ups, springs, flaps, and banners, can add extra interest to reports. What makes adding three-dimensional elements tricky is that the walls and floor move as the report opens and closes, and sometimes the elements don't fold up the way you thought they would. It's always helpful to start by lightly tacking the elements on with tape. Then, if the report closes properly, the elements can be glued down permanently. Following are four types of three-dimensional elements, presented in order of difficulty, beginning with the easiest.

- *Easiest:* **Springs and Flaps** are attached to a wall, and there is no movement when the report is opened and closed.

- *A Little Harder:* **Banners** are attached to both walls of the room and move apart as the report is opened and together as it is closed.

- *Harder:* **Wall Pop-ups** are attached to one wall and the floor. The floor moves up and down as the report closes and opens.

- *Hardest:* **Freestanding Pop-ups** are attached to the fold in the center of the floor, which moves up and down when the report opens and closes.

For durability, all of the three-dimensional elements should be created on stiffer paper. I find that 4- by-6-inch or 5- by-7-inch index cards work well. Write or draw directly on the stiff paper, or glue the illustration or writing to the stiffer paper.

Gluing Tips

There is a fair amount of stress on some of the three-dimensional elements. Those that are attached to the floor move when the report is opened or closed. When you glue the elements, make sure the tabs are covered with a thin, but solid coat of glue. Apply plenty of pressure to make sure the glue adheres.

Springs

Springs are the easiest way to attach things to the wall. They are made from two strips of paper that are folded to form an interlocking accordion strip. I like to make the springs with index cards for the added strength, but plain paper also works. I use a 1- by-4 1/4-inch strip of paper to create a spring. Your image will then stick out about a half an inch. The longer the strip, the more the illustration will pop out from the wall.

1. Lay one strip of paper (A) vertically in front of you. Glue the second strip (B) to the left edge of A, so the two form an L shape.

2. Fold A down on the top of B.

3. Fold B to the left over A.

4. Fold A up over B.

5. Fold B to the right over A.

6. Fold A down over B.

7. Fold B to the left over A and glue A and B to each other.

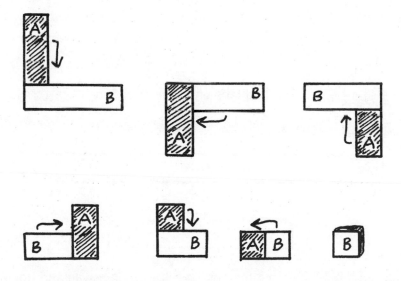

A small illustration or section of text will need one spring in the middle. A larger one can use two springs, on each side. If you use two, make sure the strips are the same length.

Flaps

Attach a flap to one of the walls to add an interactive element. Flaps can be used in a variety of ways. The flap might feature a picture on the front and a description underneath, a question on the front with the answer underneath, or a statement on the front with additional information underneath. Flaps can be a variety of shapes: rectangles, squares, etc.

To make a flap, fold a piece of paper in half. Place the fold at the top and glue the back to the wall or the floor.

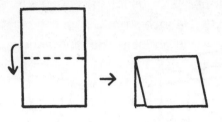

Banners

Banners stretch across the two walls of a room. They are most often used for headings and titles, but they can also have more detailed text or illustrations. Banners also work well for time lines. Banners can be made from different colors, and the edges can be shaped. Templates are included at the back of the book.

The size of the banner can vary. I usually make them 10 inches long and glue them to the walls one inch from the edge. If the length of the banner is different, the placement of the banner will need to be adjusted.

Because the walls move together as the structure closes and apart as it opens, it is best to test the mechanics by tacking the banner with tape before gluing it permanently.

1. Take a strip of paper and fold tabs under at both ends of the strip.

2. Fold the paper in half so that the tabs are facing out.

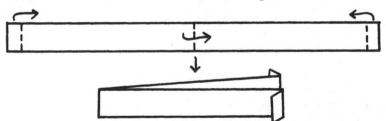

3. Put glue on the tabs, then attach one tab to the right wall and one tab to the left wall. The tabs should be about 1-inch from the outer edge of the walls. The banner should fold back into the room.

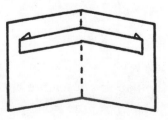

Flags, and other shapes can be attached to the banner. Glue them to either the front or the back of the banner. It's easiest if they are attached before the banner is attached to the walls. The flags can also be hung from the banner. Punch a hole in the top of the flag and thread string through, then hang from the banner. A folded piece can be attached to the center of the banner.

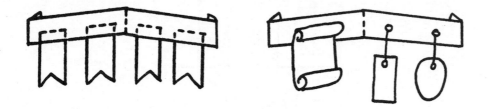

Wall Pop-ups

Wall pop-ups are placed along the wall and attached to both the floor and the wall. To create a wall pop-up, the illustration—or pop-up element—must have a tab along the bottom.

The tab is glued to the floor. The illustration is also attached to the wall with a spring. The length of the spring needs to be the same as the depth of the floor tab. If you make a 1/2-inch tab on the bottom of the illustration, use a strip of paper 1- by- 4 1/4-inches long to make the spring. If the illustration is large, you may need two springs.

1. Cut out an illustration with a 1/2-inch tab along the bottom. Fold the tab under the illustration and then unfold

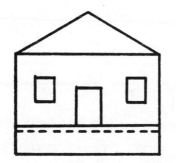

2. Apply glue to the front of the tab.

3. Line up the tab with the edge of the wall and glue to the floor. Make sure that the edge of the tab is right up against the wall. **The illustration must not extend over the fold in the center of the floor.** Press on the tab to make it adhere.

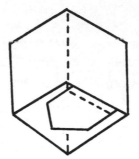

4. Make a spring from 1- by- 4 1/4-inch strips of paper. (See page 33 for directions on making springs.)

5. Glue the spring to the back of the illustration.

6. Apply glue on the other side of the spring. Lift the illustration and press it against the wall. Apply pressure to make the pop-up adhere to the wall.

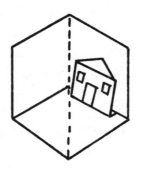

7. Gently pull the illustration from the wall to stretch out the spring.

Tips

- *Wall pop-ups cannot extend over the fold in the center of the floor.*

- *Make sure illustrations for wall pop-ups include a tab on the bottom.*

Freestanding Pop-ups

Freestanding pop-ups are glued along the fold in the center of the floor. The pop-up is folded in half vertically and attached to the floor with tabs, one on each side of the fold.

Because the floor moves when the book is opened and closed, you need to be concerned with where the pop-up is when the book is open, as well as where it is going when it is closed. When the pop-up is in the front of the room, it needs to fold back into the room when the book is closed. When the pop-up is near the back of the room, it needs to fold forward when the book is closed. If you put more than one pop-up along the fold, you need to make sure they won't crash into each other when the room is closed. You also need to be careful of hitting wall-mounted pop-ups.

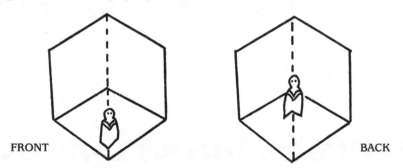

FRONT   BACK

1. Cut out the illustration, leaving a 1/2-inch tab on the bottom. Fold the tab under the illustration and then straighten it out.

2. Fold the illustration in half. If the pop-up will be at the front of the room, fold the illustration in half so that the image is facing out. If the pop-up will be at the back of the room, fold the illustration in half so that the image is on the inside.

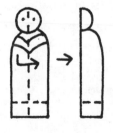

3. Cut a small triangle in the center of the tab, at the fold. You now have two tabs.

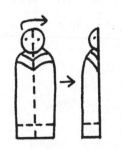

4. Apply glue to the top of the tabs.

5. Fold the tabs behind the illustration. Place the illustration on the floor so that the pop-up makes a 45-degree angle with the fold in the center of the floor. If the pop-up is at the front of the room, the angle should be behind the pop-up. If the pop-up is at the back of the room, the angle should be in front of the pop-up.

6. Close the report and open it again to make sure the pop-up works.

7. To help the glue adhere, run your finger along the top of the tabs and apply pressure from under the floor.

▲ COMMON PROBLEMS AND SOLUTIONS ▼

• **The freestanding pop-up doesn't stand up.**

This is usually because the pop-up was not glued at a 45 degree angle. When the pop-up is first glued on, it will stand up regardless of the angle. After the report is closed and then opened, it will only stand up if it is at the correct angle. I find that I can usually carefully pry the illustration off and glue it again. If you can't, you have to make another one.

• **The pop-up sticks out of the top of the report when it is closed.**

The freestanding pop-up is too far forward. Carefully pry the illustration off and glue it farther back. If you can't pry it off in one piece, you will have to make another one.

• **The pop-up hits the walls of the report when it is closed.**

The freestanding pop-up is too far back. Carefully pry the illustration off and glue the element forward. If you can't pry it off in one piece, you will have to make another one.

DESIGNING A COVER

Although the cover can be worked on at any point in the process, I prefer to save it for last. It should have the title of the report and your name. The style of the cover should reflect what is inside. It can feature one large illustration, several smaller illustrations, or just a title. If you have used a consistent style of lettering for headings in the report, use it on the cover. I think it's best to work on separate pieces of paper and glue them on the cover, just as in the report. Avoid using three-dimensional elements on the cover since they can be easily damaged. The back cover can be left plain or have additional illustrations, author information, a report summary, or a bibliography.

Protecting the Cover

To protect the cover, apply clear contact paper to the front and back covers. Another way to protect the cover is to paint the surface with clear matte medium, which is available at art supply stores, or to spray it with clear finish, which is available in hardware and art supply stores. Before you use any of these it is best to make a test sample that uses the same inks, markers, and images as the cover. There is a chance the matte medium or the clear finish spray may cause the ink or markers to bleed or in some way alter the surface.

Making a Teaching Sample

4

The following pages contain text and patterns that you can copy and cut out to make a teaching sample, which will serve as an instructional model for students. Making the teaching sample gives you an opportunity to learn the various techniques for adding two- and three-dimensional elements. I suggest making at least one sample on your own before you teach the students.

To help students understand the techniques for assembling both the buildings and creating the two- and three-dimensional elements for each room, make a second model as you work with students. Have both samples available for students to refer to as they work on putting the contents in their buildings.

ROOM A

Glue this box (B) to wall 1 below springs.

Springs

Pop-ups can be attached to the wall with springs. A small pop-up can be attached with one spring in the center. A larger one may need two springs, one on each side. Make the springs from 1- by-4 1/4-inch strips of paper

Directions for making a spring:

1. Lay one strip of paper (A) vertically in front of you. Glue the second strip (B) to the left edge of A at right angles so that they form an L.

2. Fold A down on the top of B.

3. Fold B to the left over A.

4. Fold A up over B.

5. Fold B to the right over A.

6. Fold A down over B.

7. Fold B to the left over A and glue A and B to each other.

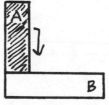

Glue this box (D) to one of the springs.

Mounting on Springs

Strip for spring

Strip for spring

Strip for spring

Strip for spring

Glue this box (A) to floor

All of the illustrations and writing are done on separate sheets of paper and then glued into the book.

Create the background for each room with colored or patterned paper. The illustrations can be your own drawings, photographs cut from magazines, photocopies colored with colored pencils, maps, and more! The text can be written by hand or typed on a computer. Try writing on colored paper or mount the text on colored paper. Experiment and have fun!

Make two springs using the four paper strips 1-by-4 1/4 inches. Glue to wall 1 above instructions on making springs.

Fold (E) in half and glue to wall 2.

Front of Flap

Glue (C) to wall 2.

Flaps

Flaps can be attached to the wall or floor as a way of adding an interactive element. Use the top for the flap and the underneath for additional information. The flaps can be used in a variety of ways: with a picture on the flap and a description underneath, text on the flap with a picture underneath, or a statement on the flap and an explanation underneath.

Directions for making a flap:

1. Fold a piece of paper in half.

2. Place the fold at the top.

3. Glue the back of the flap to the wall or floor

ROOM B

Glue this box (A) to the floor.

Banners

Banners are attached to each wall and stretch across the room. Because the walls move together as the structure closes and apart as it opens, it is best to test the mechanics by tacking the banner with tape before gluing it permanently. The size of the banner can vary. I usually make them 10 inches long and glue them to the walls 1-inch from the edge. If the length is different, the banner will need to be glued a different distance from the edge. Banners are most often used for headings and titles, but they can also have more detailed text or illustrations. Banners also work well for time lines. They can be made from different colors. The edges can be scalloped or altered.

Other pieces of paper can be attached to the banners. It's easier if they are attached to the banner before the banner is attached to the wall.

Directions for making a banner:

1. Fold the two end tabs under. These will be glued to the wall.

2. Fold the banner in half so that the tabs are on the outside.

3. Open, put glue on the tabs, and glue them to the walls about 1 1/2 inch from the outer edges. The banner should extend back into the room.

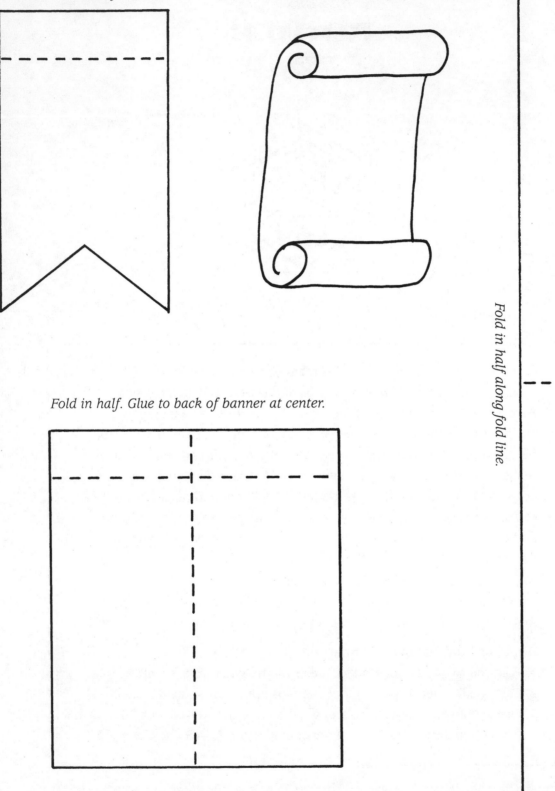

Glue to the back of banner.

Glue to the front of the banner.

Fold in half. Glue to back of banner at center.

Fold in half along fold line.

▲ ROOM C ▼

Glue this box (A) to the floor

✂ ------------------------

As you work on wall and freestanding pop-ups, you need to make sure that they will function properly when the book is both open and closed. You will be working with the book open. Sometimes you may find that the pop-up looks and works great until you close the book. I usually tape the pop-ups in and close the book. If they work, I glue them in.

Glue (B) to wall 1

Wall Pop-ups

To create a wall pop-up, the illustration is glued to the floor and attached to the wall with a spring. The illustration should have a 1/2-inch tab, which is glued to the floor. Remember to plan for this as you draw and cut out your illustration. The length of the spring needs to be the same depth as the floor tab. If you make a 1/2-inch tab on the bottom of the illustration, use two strips of paper, each 1- by- 4 1/4-inches long, to make the spring. If the illustration is large, you may need two springs.

Strips for springs

Glue (C) to wall 2

Directions for Creating Wall Pop-ups:

1. Cut out illustration with a 1/2-inch tab along the bottom. Fold the tab under the illustration and then unfold.
2. Apply glue to the top of the tab.
3. Glue the tab to the floor so that the edge of the tab is right up against the wall. The illustration must not extend over the fold in the center of the floor.
4. Lay the illustration down and press on the tab to make it adhere.
5. Make a spring from 1- by- 4 1/4-inch strips of paper.
6. Glue the spring to the back of the illustration.
7. Apply glue to the other side of the spring.
8. Stand the illustration up and press against the wall and smooth with pressure to make the spring adhere to the wall.
9. Gently pull the illustration from the wall to stretch out the spring.

Caution: The illustration cannot overlap the fold in the center of the floor or the report will not close.

Strips for springs

Make springs and use to attach illustration to wall 1.

Glue the house to floor at wall 1.

ROOM D

Glue (A) to wall 1

Freestanding Pop-ups

Freestanding pop-ups are attached to the floor. The pop-ups are folded in half, and glued along the fold in the center of the floor. The pop-up is attached to the floor with tabs, one on each side of the fold.

Because the floor moves when the report is closed, you need to be concerned with where the pop-up is when the report is open as well as where it is going when it is closed. When the pop-up is in the front of the room, it needs to fold back into the room when the book is closed. When the pop-up is in the back of the room, it needs to fold forward when the book is closed. If you put more than one pop-up along the fold, you need to make sure they don't crash into each other when the room is closed. You also need to be careful of hitting wall-mounted pop-ups.

Glue (B) to wall 2

✂

Directions for Making a Freestanding Pop-up

1. Draw and cut out illustration with a 1/2-inch tab on the bottom.

2. Fold the tab under the illustration and then straighten it out.

3. Fold the illustration in half.

4. Create two tabs by cutting a small triangle in the tab at the center of the tab.

Attaching the Pop-up

1. Fold the illustration in half. If the pop-up will be at the front of the room, fold the illustration so that the image is facing out. If the pop-up will be at the back of the room, fold the illustration so that the image is on the inside.

2. Fold the tab behind the illustration. Place it on the floor so that the pop-up makes a 45-degree angle with the fold in the center of the floor. If the pop-up is at the front of the room, the angle should be behind the pop-up. If the pop-up is at the back of the room, the angle should be in front of the pop-up.

Glue to floor

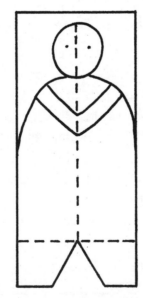
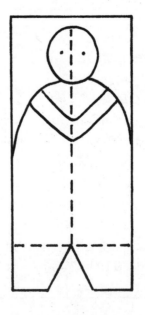

Topics and Templates
5

The following section is divided into eight parts, one for each of the topic areas: Native Americans, Explorers, Colonial America, the Revolutionary War, the Underground Railroad, Pioneers, the Civil War, and Immigration. Each section contains suggested themes and topics for the reports, suggested resources and readings, and reproducible templates.

Themes

The suggested themes are here to get you started. For each section, I have taken one or two topics and shown how they can be divided into four subject areas, one for each room. I have also listed additional topic ideas. History does not divide itself as neatly as this book tries to do. I have therefore made some artificial divisions. For example, I have placed abolition and slavery with the Underground Railroad instead of the Civil War.

Points of View

In addition to presenting their research in a traditional manner, students might try adopting the point of view of a historical figure. For example, a report on explorers might be written in Columbus's voice, and have a room explaining his early life, a room explaining his plans for the trip, a room detailing the journey, and a room with his reactions to reaching land. Another option is for students to use each room to report on a historical event from a different person's perspective. In a report on the Revolutionary War, one room could show the experience of a British soldier, with an illustration of his uniform, a description of British battle tactics, and the feelings of a British soldier fighting a war far from home. Another room could focus on a Tory with an explanation of why he supported continued ties with Britain and the difficulties of taking that position. Another room could show a Continental soldier and talk about the hardships, the reasons for fighting, and the style of fighting. The fourth room could show a supporter of the Patriot cause or someone who remained neutral.

Templates

Each section features reproducible templates that students can cut out and use for their reports. The templates are not intended to replace students gathering and making their own images. I would be thrilled if your students drew and collected all their own pictures and never used the templates. However, I understand that some students have difficulty with drawing, and the templates are here to help.

I've tried to include basic images for each topic area and students are free to select and adapt templates from different sections to meet their needs. For example, in a report on the Pilgrims, students can incorporate images from the Native American section.

The patterns can be reproduced on a copier and cut out. Templates can also be reduced or enlarged on a copier. Any figures that will pop up from the wall or pop up from the floor should be mounted on a heavier-weight paper.

Students can also trace any templates they like and then personalize the illustrations to their liking. For example, if they like a figure of a woman but want her to have a different hat, they can trace the figure and change the hat.

Resources

Each topic area includes a listing of books and Web sites that I have found helpful. I looked for material that offered both visual and written resources. A particularly useful resource for American history is the series *The History of the US* by Joy Hakim (Oxford University Press), which presents history in a very readable and accessible format.

Suggested Reading

I have listed two titles of fiction to accompany each section. My choices are based on the recommendations of librarians, teachers, and students, as well as my own personal taste. The *Dear America* series from Scholastic includes titles on many key American history topics

▲ NATIVE AMERICANS ▼

Suggested Themes

◆ Traditional Life: focusing on an individual tribe or the tribes of an area

   1. Home: food, clothing, shelter, heat and light, entertainment

   2. Religion: beliefs, celebrations and ceremonies

   3. Work: hunter, gatherer, farmer, transportation

   4. Arts and Crafts

Points of View

◆ Native Americans: Sachem or chief, shaman or medicine man, woman, man, adolescent boy or girl, young child, elder

◆ Settlers, Calvary, U.S. Government, Spanish settlers and explorers

Other Topics

◆ Ancient cultures: Anasazi (Southwest), Mound Builders (Ohio), Aztec and Maya (Mexico and Central America), Inca (Peru)

◆ Iroquois Confederacy

◆ Sequoyah and the Cherokee alphabet

◆ Trail of Tears

◆ The Long Walk of the Navajo

◆ Little Bighorn

◆ Wounded Knee

◆ Biographies of famous Native Americans: Sequoyah, Chief Joseph, Geronimo, Sitting Bull, Red Cloud, Crazy Horse, Cochise, Black Hawk, Sacajawea

Resources

The Encyclopedia of Native America, by Trudy Griffin-Pierce (Viking, 1995). An overview of native America by regions, with maps, illustrations, an informative text.

This Web site (http://www. dickshovel.com/up.html) features information on language, population, names, culture, and history for a long list of Native American tribes.

Native American Resources (http://hanksville.phast.umass.edu/misc/indices/ NAculture.html) includes links to a large number of Native American sites.

Suggested Reading

Sees Behind Trees, by Michael Dorris (Hyperion Books, 1996). Walnut, an Indian boy in Virginia, earns his adult name, Sees Behind Trees, because he has learned to compensate for his poor eyesight by developing his other senses. As he tries to understand the world of adults and his place in it, he accompanies Gray Fire, a tribal elder, on a mysterious journey that brings as many questions as answers.

Sing Down the Moon, by Scott O'Dell (Houghton Mifflin Company, 1970). Bright Morning, a young Navaho woman, recounts the tragedy she and her people meet when the white soldiers, called Long Knives, remove them from the Canyon de Chelly in New Mexico in 1864.

Hopi with
squash blossom
hairstyle
of an unmarried
girl

Iroquois
man

Nez Perce
young woman

Dakota
warrior

Seminole
woman

Bella Coola man
in ceremonial
dress

Buffalo

Pueblo

Hopi
kachina doll

Above, Border design based on Mohegan beadwork pattern; Below, Border design based on Navajo woman's blanket

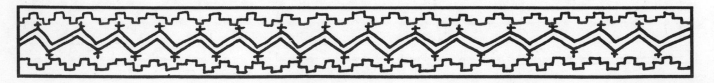

Totem Pole

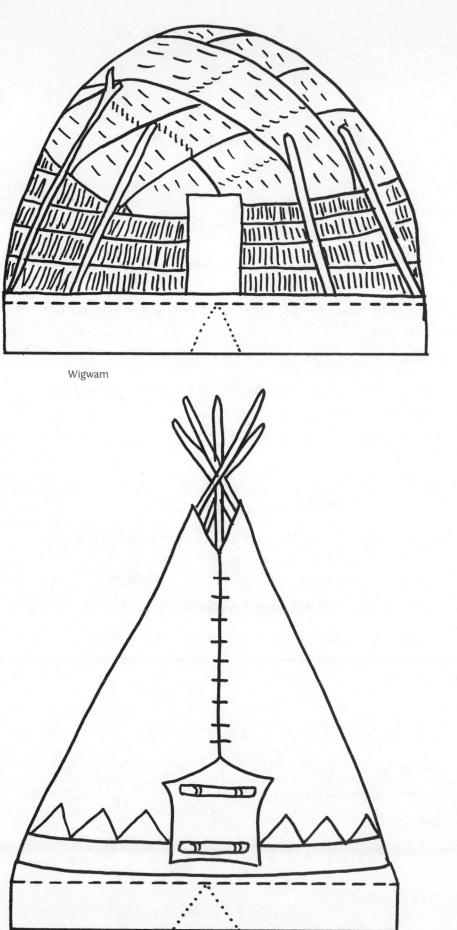

Wigwam

Tipi

Pottery bowl or basket
(add decorations or design)

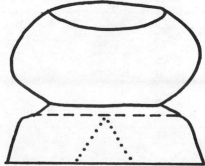

55

▲ EXPLORERS ▼

Suggested Themes

◆ The Explorer's Journey: an overview of exploration or a report on a specific explorer

    1. In Europe: who sponsored the explorer and what were the sponsor's motivations?

    2. Voyage: name and type of ship, route taken, length of trip, conditions

    3. Arrival: where they landed, what the land and climate were like, who they met, what kind of reception they received

    4. What happened next: what the explorer did once he arrived, and the results of the expedition

Points of View

◆ Monarch sponsoring the journey, European nobility, European peasants, European merchants, explorer, explorer's crew, Native Americans

Other Topics

◆ Early navigation: using the North Star for direction, using the astrolabe and quadrant for latitude, compasses, dragging a log (dead reckoning) for determining longitude

◆ Ships

◆ Prince Henry's School of Navigation (1450)

◆ The four voyages of Columbus

◆ Impact of the explorers on Native Americans

◆ Viking explorations

◆ West coast exploration: James Cook in 1778, Juan Perez in 1774

◆ Discoveries made by explorers, including food, plants, animals and medicine brought back to Europe.

◆ Biographies of famous explorers: John Cabot, Sebastian Cabot, Jacques Cartier, Christopher Columbus, James Cook, Leif Ericson, Henry Hudson, Sieur de La Salle, Amerigo Vespucci, Hernando De Soto, Cortes

Resources

Discoverer's Web (http://www.win.tue.nl/cs/fm/engels/discovery) includes a wealth of information and links.

Suggested Readings

Morning Girl, by Michael Dorris (Hyperion Books, 1992). Told in the first person by Morning Girl and Star Boy, Morning Girl describes the family life of the Taino on a Bahamian island in 1492, ending with the arrival of Columbus.

Pedro's Journal, A Voyage with Christopher Columbus, by Pam Conrad (Caroline House, 1991). Pedro de Salcedo, ship's boy on Columbus's first voyage, describes in his journal the journey, the sighting of land, and the interactions between Columbus's men and the native inhabitants.

Viking

Christopher
Columbus

Jacques
Cartier

Spanish
Conquistador

Aztec
warrior

Carib

58

Map

Viking ship

Astrolabe
(used for navigation)

Above, Wave-pattern border; Below, Border with design based on compass rose

Santa Maria, Columbus' ship

Crest for England

Crest for Spain

Crest for the Netherlands

Crest for Portugal

Crest for France

60

▲ COLONIAL AMERICA ▼

Suggested Themes

◆ Colonial America: focus on one colony or compare four

1. Reasons for settling in colony

2. Voyage

3. Earliest days of the colony

4. Later settlement in the colony

◆ Daily Life in the Colonies: Choose one colony or compare New England, Middle, and Southern colonies by category.

1. Home: food, clothing, shelter, entertainment, religion

2. Education

3. Work: agriculture, crafts and trades, tools

4. Transportation

Points of View

◆ Pilgrims, Puritans, small farmers, wealthy landowners, slaves, women, children, artisans, Native Americans

Other Topics

◆ Relations between the colonists and the Native Americans: Jamestown and Powhatan or Plymouth and Squanto

◆ King Philip's War

◆ Triangular trade

◆ French and Indian War

◆ Biographies of famous figures from the Colonial period: John Smith, Pocahontas, Powhatan, John Winthrop, William Bradford, Squanto, Massasoit, King Philip, Miles Standish, Ann Hutchinson, Roger Williams, William Penn, Peter Stuyvesant, James Oglethorpe, Ben Franklin

Resources

Colonial Williamsburg's Web site (http://www.colonialwilliamsburg.org) features a great deal of information on life in Colonial America.

The Plymoth Plantation's Web site (http://www.plimoth.org) includes information on the Pilgrims and life in Plymouth.

Colonial Living, by Edwin Tunis (Thomas Y. Crowell Company, 1957). Lots of detailed pen-and-ink illustrations on Colonial life by area and time period.

Drama of American History, by Christopher Collier and James Lincoln Collier (Benchmark Books). A series that focuses on broad themes of Colonial life rather than specific events, and covers the clash of cultures between the early settlers and the Native Americans to the American Revolution.

Suggested Readings

Call Me Regina, by Sally M. Keehn (Philomel Books, 1991). In this harrowing story, 12-year-old Regina is by Indians and taken from her home in Pennsylvania, 12-year-old Regina is taken to live with Tiger Claw and his mother, Woelfin. She slowly becomes Tskinnak and builds a new life and identity in the village, only to have her identity questioned again when she is taken back by white soldiers.

The Witch of Blackbird Pond, by Elizabeth George Speare (Houghton Mifflin Company, 1958). This classic retains its sparkle as a great read filled with suspense, adventure, and romance. Spirited Kit Tyler, raised in luxury in Barbados, experiences a very different life when she comes to live with her aunt, uncle, and two cousins in Connecticut in 1687.

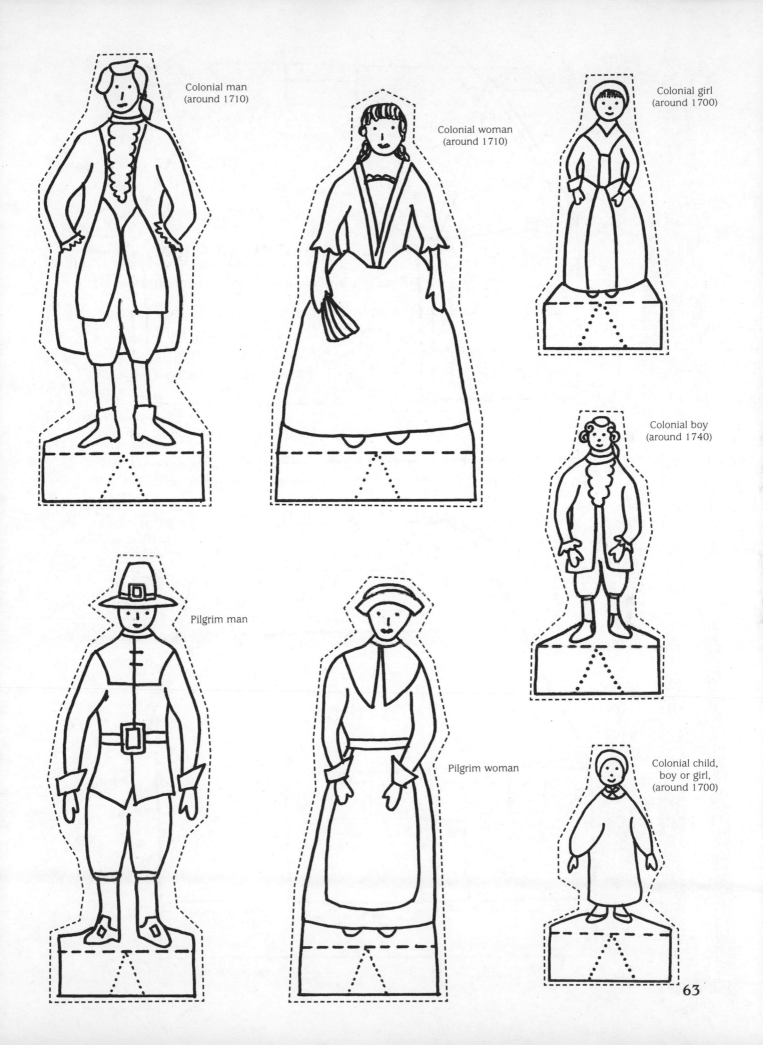

Colonial man
(around 1710)

Colonial woman
(around 1710)

Colonial girl
(around 1700)

Colonial boy
(around 1740)

Pilgrim man

Pilgrim woman

Colonial child,
boy or girl,
(around 1700)

63

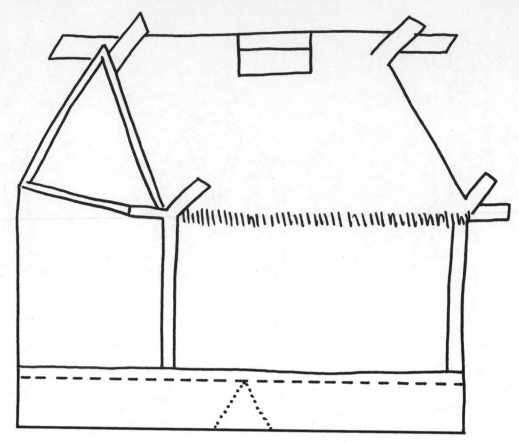

Early Jamestown dwelling with wattle and daub walls and a thatched roof

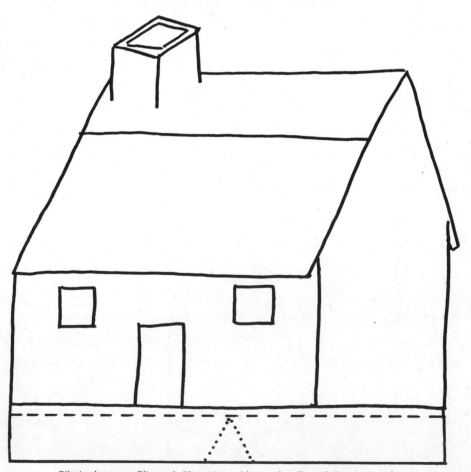

Pilgrim house at Plimouth Plantation with wood walls and thatched roof

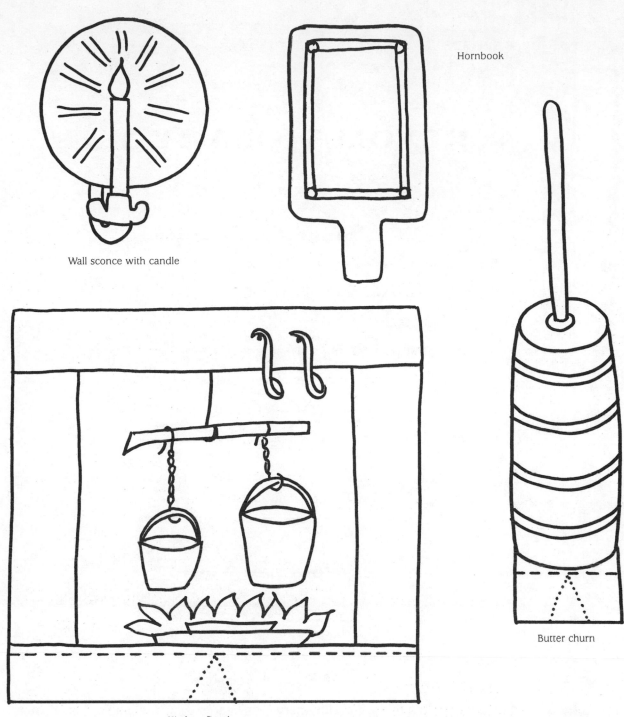

Wall sconce with candle

Hornbook

Butter churn

Kitchen fireplace

Above, Border based on acorn-and-oak wallpaper pattern; Below, Border of pineapple (the symbol of hospitality in Colonial times)

▲ REVOLUTIONARY WAR ▼

Suggested Themes

◆ The American Revolution

1. Causes and events leading to the war

2. Start of the war

3. Fighting the war: fighting styles, battles

4. The end of the war: surrender at Yorktown

◆ The Soldier's Life: focus on the Continental or British soldier

1. Uniforms and weapons

2. Camp life

3. In battle: fighting styles

4. Generals

Points of View

◆ Tory, Patriot, British soldier in America, Hessian soldier, Continental soldier, slaves, free African-Americans, Native Americans

Other Topics

◆ Events leading to the Revolutionary War: Stamp Act, Intolerable Acts, Boston Massacre, Boston Tea Party

◆ The Declaration of Independence

◆ Famous battles: Lexington and Concord, Ticonderoga, Bunker Hill, Long Island, Harlem Heights, White Plains, Trenton, Princeton, Saratoga, Brandywine, Monmouth, King's Mountain, Cowpens, Guilford Court House, Yorktown

◆ Paul Revere's ride

◆ Winter at Valley Forge

◆ Lafayette and the French in the Revolution

◆ John Paul Jones and the naval war

◆ Biographies of famous figures during the American Revolution: Samuel Adams, John Adams, Paul Revere, Thomas Jefferson, Benjamin Franklin, George Washington, Crispus Attucks, Thomas Paine, Nathan Hale, Patrick Henry, Betsy Ross, Molly Pitcher, Phyllis Wheatley

Resources

The American Revolution Links Web site (http://www.n-polk.k12.ia.us/Depart-ments/media/amerev.html) is just what it says, lots of links to American Revolution Web sites.

Suggested Readings

Johnny Tremain, by Esther Forbes (Houghton Mifflin Company, 1943). Written more than 50 years ago, this story still brings alive the excitement and passion of the Patriot cause in Boston. Johnny's life as a skilled and proud apprentice is shattered when he is injured in the silversmith's shop where he works. He rebuilds his life when he becomes involved in the events that lead to the battle of Lexington.

My Brother Sam Is Dead, by James Lincoln Collier and Christopher Collier (Four Winds Press, 1974) While Johnny Tremain sweeps us along with passionate ideals about freedom, *My Brother Sam Is Dead*—by telling the story of Tim Meeker, son of a Tory and brother of a Continental soldier—questions the price paid in individual lives.

Continental
Infantryman

British soldier

Hessian
Grenadier
officer

Continental
seaman

Colonial
woman helping
in battle

Continental drummer boy

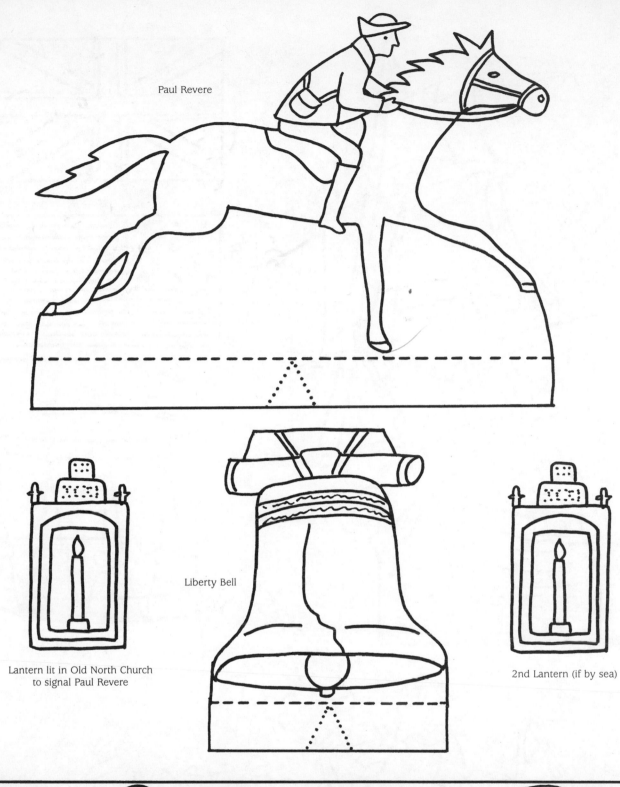

Paul Revere

Lantern lit in Old North Church
to signal Paul Revere

Liberty Bell

2nd Lantern (if by sea)

Above, Border design based on Ben Franklin's political cartoon, Join or die; Below, Border design of eagle, symbol of the United States

British flag

U.S.S.
Constitution

Most
commonly
used U.S.
Flag during
Revolution

Drum

Washington crossing the Delaware, December 25, 1776

▲ PIONEERS ▼

Suggested Themes

◆ The Pioneer's Journey

   1. Why they left and what they left behind

   2. The Journey West: transportation, trails followed, clothing, food

   3. The Journey West: hardships and difficulties

   4. The Frontier

Points of View

◆ Pioneer woman, man, child, family members who stayed behind, Native Americans, cowboys, explorers,

Other Topics

◆ Pioneer transportation: horse, wagon, stagecoach, canal barge, steamboat, handcart, railroad

◆ Inventions that helped settle the West: telegraph, steam locomotive, farm machinery

◆ Lewis and Clark expedition

◆ The Donner Party

◆ California gold rush

◆ Brigham Young and the Mormons in Utah

◆ Louisiana Purchase

◆ Cowboys

◆ Pony Express

◆ The buffalo

◆ Oregon Trail, Sante Fe Trail

◆ Erie Canal

◆ Biographies of famous pioneers: Meriwether Lewis, William Clark, John James Audubon, Francis Parkman, General George Custer, Laura Ingalls Wilder, John Chapman (Johnny Appleseed), Zebulon Pike

Resources

Children of the Wild West, by Russell Freedman (Clarion Books, 1984). A well-illustrated guide to life in the West for children.

Frontier Living, by Edwin Tunis (Thomas Y. Crowell Company, 1961). Features detailed pen-and-ink illustrations on frontier life by area and time period.

Pioneers, by Martin W. Sandler (HarperCollins, 1994.) A Library of Congress book with great images and a simple informative text.

New Perspectives on the West Web site (http://www.pbs.org/weta/thewest), is a companion to the PBS series "The West," and includes a sampling of the history of the West with time line, map, biographies, and links to related sites.

Suggested Readings

The Ballad of Lucy Whipple, by Karen Cushman (Clarion Books, 1996). Feisty California Morning Whipple leaves Massachusetts in 1849 and journeys with her mother, brother, and two sisters west to California. Unlike the rest of her family, who make the best of a difficult life running a boarding house in a tent town called Lucky Diggins, California changes her name to Lucy and longs for home. It's great fun to see the California gold rush through her eyes and to watch her grow into an independent young woman who finds her place in the West.

Prairie Songs, by Pam Conrad (Harper & Row, 1985). Life changes for Louisa Downing and her family when a doctor brings his beautiful wife, Emmeline, from New York to live in a sod house on the Nebraska prairie. Louisa has a window onto the adult world as the story of Emmeline's inability to adapt to her new surroundings unfolds. This poignant story uses a spare poetic language to communicate the loneliness of the prairie and the stoic spirit of its inhabitants.

Pioneer woman

Pioneer man

Pioneer boy

Prospector

Cowboy

Pioneer girl

73

Conestoga wagon

Leather tar bucket (use to
hold pine tar and grease
to grease the wagon
wheels)

Steam engine

Plow

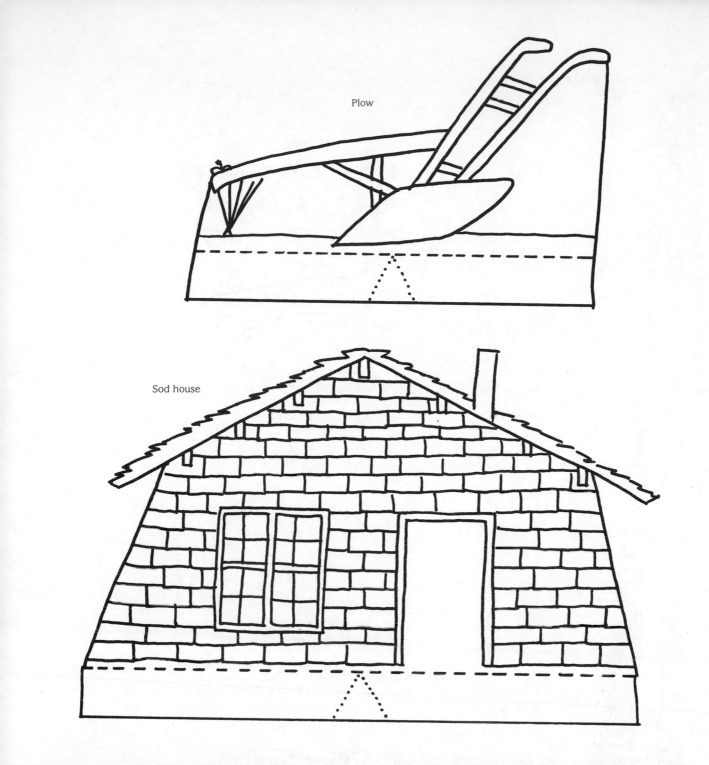

Sod house

Above, Border design of wagon wheels; Below, Border design based on a patchwork quilt pattern

▲ THE UNDERGROUND RAILROAD ▼

Suggested Themes

◆ Journey to Freedom

   1. Life of a slave

   2. Traveling the Underground Railroad in the South

   3. Traveling the Underground Railroad: in the North

   4. Destination and life after arrival

◆ The Life of a Slave

   1. Life in Africa

   2. Capture in Africa

   3. The middle passage

   4. Life as a slave

Points of View

◆ Slave owner, free African-American, slave who escapes, slave who escapes and is caught, slave who stays on the plantation, conductor, stationmaster, abolitionist

Other Topics

◆ Amistad

◆ Fugitive Slave Bill of 1850

◆ John Brown's raid on Harper Ferry

◆ The abolitionists

◆ Nat Turner's rebellion

◆ Biographies of prominent figures in the Underground Railroad: Harriet Tubman, Sojourner Truth, Frederick Douglass, William Lloyd Garrison, Harriet Beecher Stowe, John Brown, Nat Turner, Abraham Lincoln

Resources

Many Thousand Gone: African Americans from Slavery to Freedom, by Virginia Hamilton, illustrated by Leo and Diane Dillon (Alfred A. Knopf, 1992). Brief histories of African-Americans in American history.

The Menare Foundation's North Star (http://www.ugrr.org/wwwhome.html) is a Web site by Anthony Cohen, who re-created an Underground Railroad journey from Alabama to Canada.

Suggested Readings

Nightjohn, by Gary Paulsen (Delacorte, 1993). Twelve-year-old Sarny, a slave, tells how she is taught to read by Nightjohn, an escaped slave who returns to bondage to teach others to read. This is a short book that packs a lot of punch. Written in dialect, it vividly describes life in the slave quarters in all its brutality, while portraying the bravery and dignity of the inhabitants. *Sarny, a Life Remembered* is the sequel to this story.

True North, by Kathryn Lasky (The Blue Sky Press, 1996). True North tells in alternating chapters the stirring stories of two girls until their lives intersect at the end. Lucy Wentworth Bradford is a free spirit in a conventional, wealthy Boston family whose only ally is her beloved grandfather. Afrika is a slave who escapes with Harriet Tubman but makes the journey North alone. *True North* gives a view of slave life, the Underground Railroad, Northern life, and the abolitionist movement.

Woman traveling on the Underground Railroad

Man traveling on the Underground Railroad

Boy traveling on the Underground Railroad

Slave patrol to catch runaway slaves

Conductor (many of whom were Quakers)

Girl traveling on the Underground Railroad

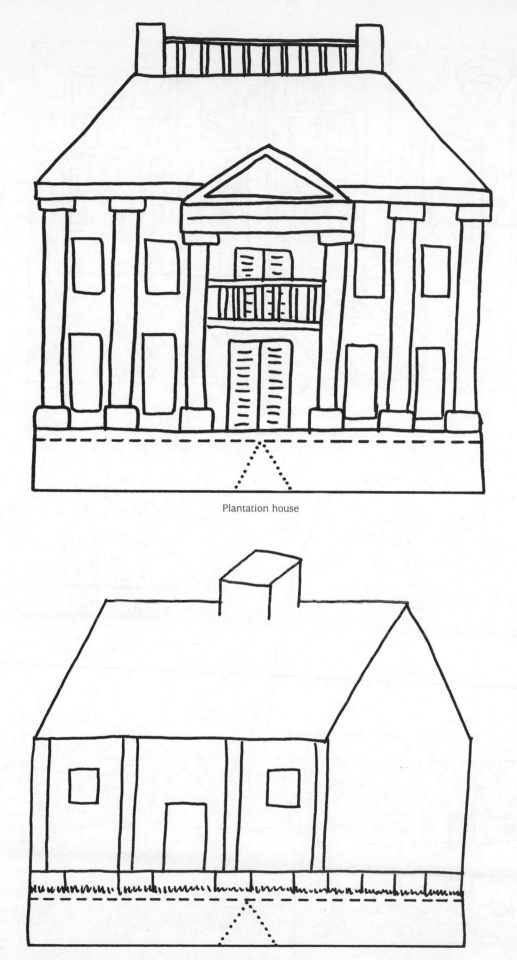

Plantation house

Slave quarters

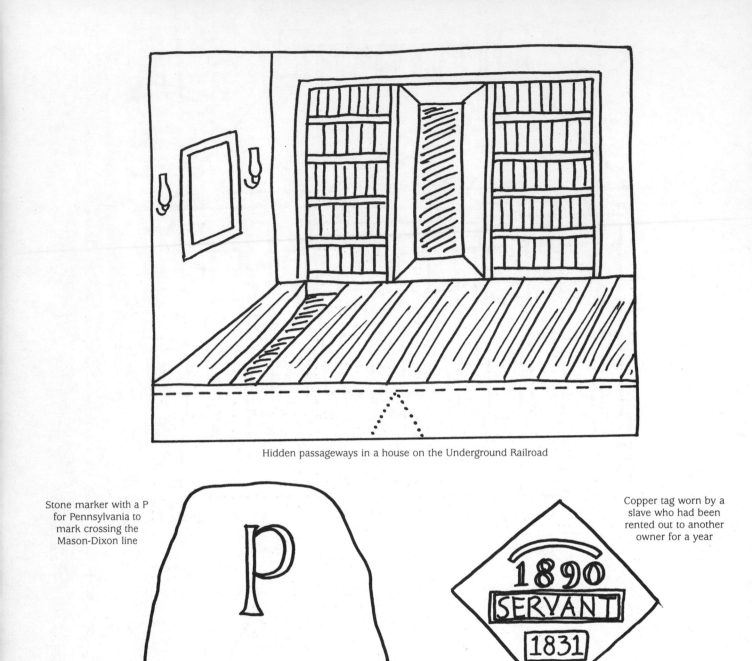

Hidden passageways in a house on the Underground Railroad

Stone marker with a P for Pennsylvania to mark crossing the Mason-Dixon line

Copper tag worn by a slave who had been rented out to another owner for a year

1890 SERVANT 1831

Above, Border design of a stream. (Water hid the scent from the dogs who were chasing the escaping slaves.)
Below, Border design based on North Star (which guided travelers on the Underground Railroad)

THE CIVIL WAR

Suggested Themes

◆ The Civil War

  1. Causes

  2. First battle at Fort Sumter

  3. Overview of the war: major battles

  4. Surrender at Appomatox

◆ The Soldier's life

1.-2. Camp life: food, clothing, shelter, weather, training, boredom and entertainment, letters home

  3. Battles

  4. Hospitals and medicine: treatments and medical advances during the war

Points of View

◆ Union soldier, Confederate soldier, Union Officer, Confederate officer, nurse, doctor, boy drummer or soldier, Union and Confederate mothers and wives, slave, free African-American, abolitionist

Other Topics

◆ Missouri Compromise, Kansas-Nebraska Act, Dred Scott decision, John Brown's raid, publication of Uncle Tom's cabin, Lincoln-Douglas Debates, Election of Lincoln

◆ Battles: First Manassas, Second Manassas, Antietam, Fredericksburg, Shiloh, Chancellorsville, Gettysburg, Vicksburg, Chickamauga, Chattanooga, Atlanta, Wilderness, Spotsylvania Courthouse, Cold Harbor, Sherman's March, Franklin, Petersburg, Nashville, Appomatox

◆ The Naval War: blockade and blockade runners, battle of the *Merrimack* and the *Monitor*

◆ Biographies of important Civil War figures: Abraham Lincoln, Jefferson Davis, Ulysses S. Grant, Robert E. Lee, Stonewall Jackson, Robert Gould Shaw, William Tecumseh Sherman, Nathan Bedford Forrest, Clara Barton, Matthew Brady

Resources

Civil War, by Martin W. Sandler (HarperCollins, 1996). A Library of Congress book with great images and a simple informative text.

The American Civil War homepage. (http://sunsite.utk.edu/civil-war/warweb.html), from the University of Tennessee, includes many links to a variety of Civil War Web sites.

Civil War Gazette (http://www.itdc.sbcss.k12.ca.us/curriculum/civilwar.html) is a Web quest project for students interested in creating a Civil War newspaper, includes links to original Civil War material.

Suggested Readings

Charley Skedaddle, by Patricia Beatty (William Morrow,1987). Twelve-year-old Charley Quinn, a New York Bowery Boy, joins the Union Army as a drummer boy to fight the Rebels who killed his brother Johnny at Gettysburg. Frightened in his first battle, he "skedaddles" west to the mountains, where he regains his sense of self through tests of man and nature. The soldiering scenes are vivid, and Charley's growth to responsibility and strength is a moving one.

Turn Homeward, Hannalee, by Patricia Beatty (William Morrow,1984). Twelve-year-old Hannalee Reed, a bobbin girl in a mill in Georgia, is captured by the Yankees and taken north by the Union Army to work in the northern mills. Full of determination and pluck, she disguises herself as a boy, runs away, finds her brother, and makes the long journey back to Georgia. Through Hannalee's journey, we see the war's terrible effect on both sides.

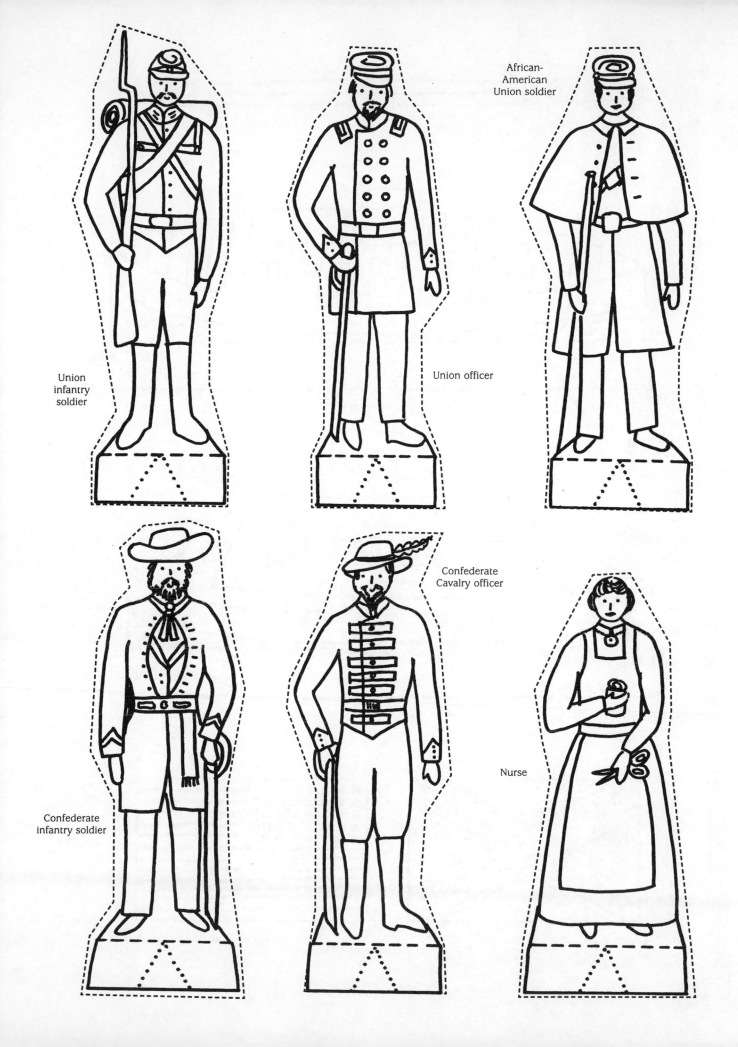

Union
infantry
soldier

Union officer

African-
American
Union soldier

Confederate
Cavalry officer

Confederate
infantry soldier

Nurse

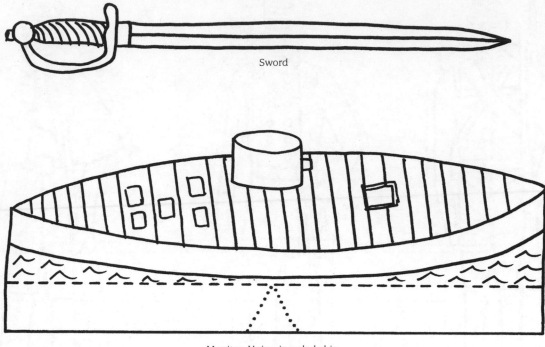

Sword

Monitor, Union ironclad ship

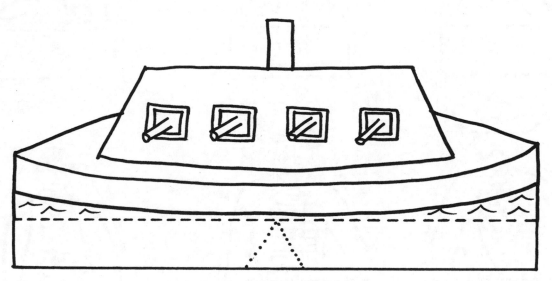

Merrimack, Confederate ironclad ship

Confederate Flag

Most common Union flag, used from 1836

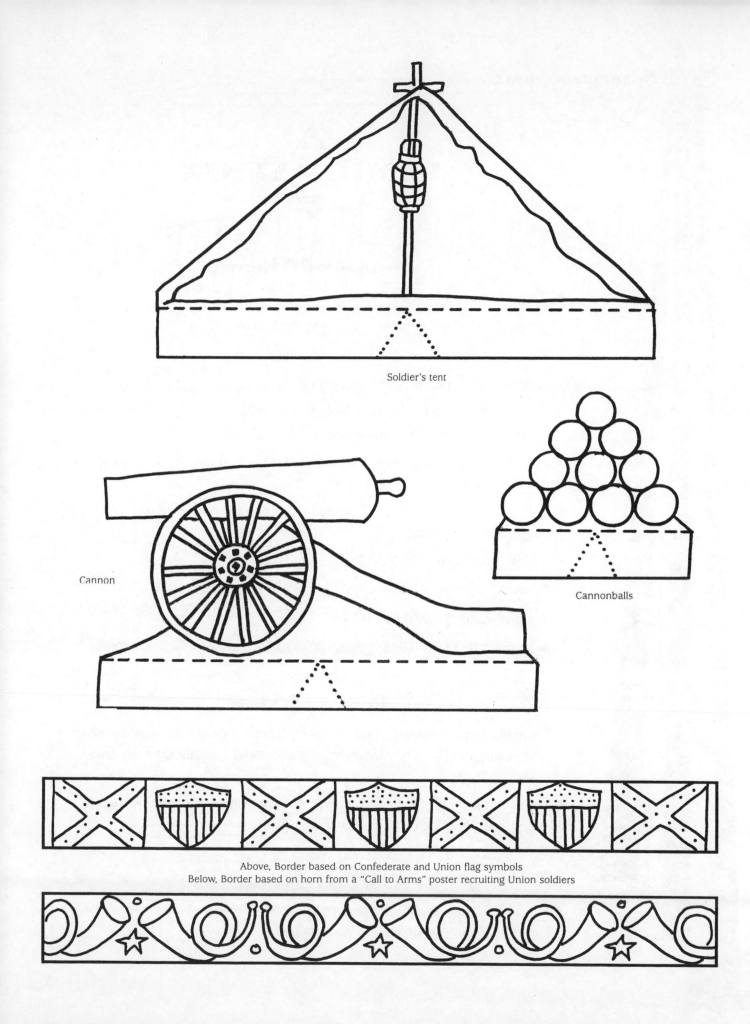

Soldier's tent

Cannon

Cannonballs

Above, Border based on Confederate and Union flag symbols
Below, Border based on horn from a "Call to Arms" poster recruiting Union soldiers

▲ IMMIGRATION ▼

Suggested Themes

◆ The Immigrant's Journey

   1. Life in the original country and reasons for emigrating

   2. Journey: transportation, conditions, length of time

   3. Arrival: requirements and process for entering

   4. Life in America: where they settled, what they did for a living, how they were treated by other Americans

◆ Four Immigrants: Each room can tell the story of an immigrant from a different country

◆ Immigration by Time Periods: predominant groups, how they traveled, where they settled, reception

   1. Immigration from 1600–1830

   2. Immigration from 1830–1890,

   3. Immigration from 1890–1924,

   4. Immigration from 1968–present

Points of View

◆ Immigrant man, woman, child, people left behind (such as a grandmother whose son and his family leave) immigration agent, established American citizen

◆ Points of Entry: Castle Garden, NY; Ellis Island, New York Harbor; Angel Island, San Francisco Harbor, Statue of Liberty

Other Topics

◆ Life after immigration: tenement housing (New York and other cities), Farming (Scandinavians in the Midwest), Chinatowns

◆ Irish Potato Famine

◆ Killing Fields of Cambodia

◆ Cuban migration after Castro

Resources

Ellis Island: Through America's Gateway (http://www.ellisisland.org) is a Web site that includes a tour of Ellis Island and explains the processing of immigrants.

Immigrants, by Martin W. Sandler (HarperCollins, 1995). A Library of Congress book with great images and a simple, informative text.

Immigrant Kids, by Russell Freedman (Clarion Books, 1980). A series of interviews with immigrants to the United States.

Suggested Readings

Dragonwings, by Laurence Yep (Harper and Row Publishers, 1975). In 1903, nine-year-old Shadow Moon journeys from China to San Francisco to join his father, Windrider, whom he has never seen. As he grows up in the Land of the Golden Mountain, he assists his father in his dream to build a flying machine like the Wright brothers.

Letters from Rifka, by Karen Hesse (Henry Holt and Company, 1992). This series of letters, written by Rifka Nebrot, a Russian Jew, to her cousin Tovah, chronicles Rifka's escape from Russia and the long, difficult journey through Europe and across the Atlantic to Ellis Island.

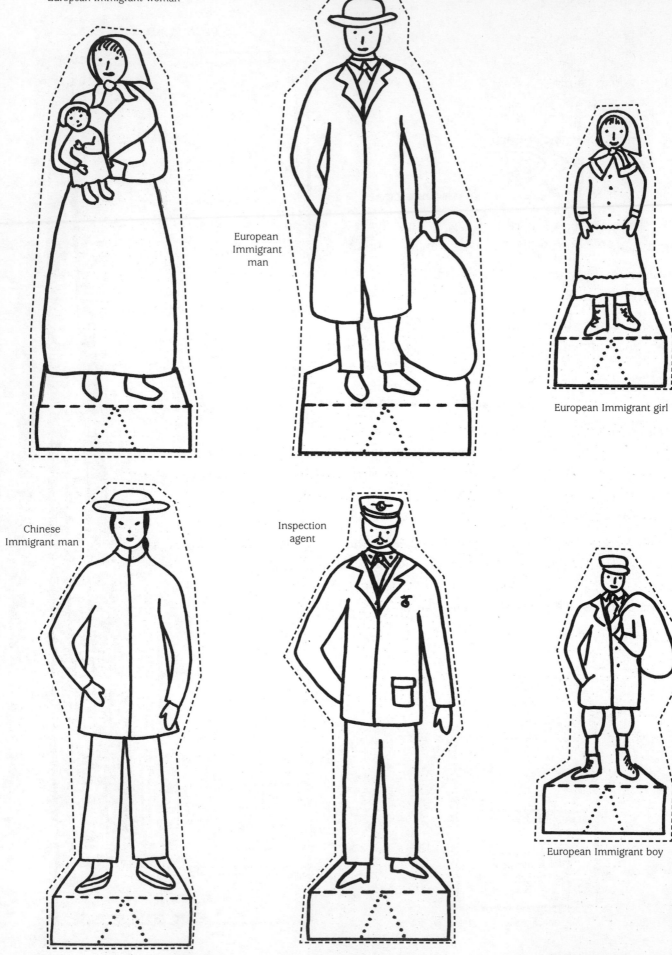

European Immigrant woman

European
Immigrant
man

European Immigrant girl

Chinese
Immigrant man

Inspection
agent

European Immigrant boy

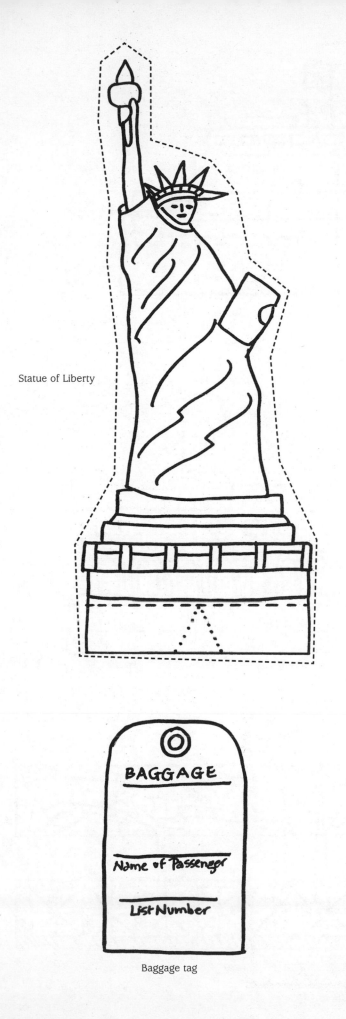

Statue of Liberty

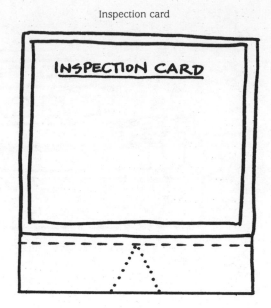

Inspection card

INSPECTION CARD

Tenement house

BAGGAGE

Name of Passenger

List Number

Baggage tag

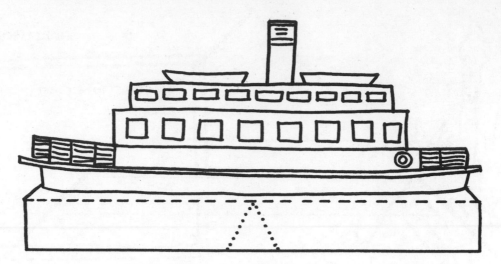

Ferry to Ellis Island from Castle Garden where ships from Europe docked

Buildings at Ellis Island

Below Border design based on advertising posters for White Star Line (one of the main shipping lines transporting immigrants from Europe)

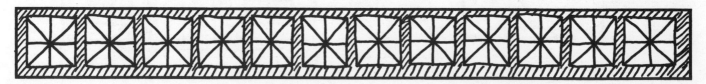

Above, Border design based on windows at Ellis Island

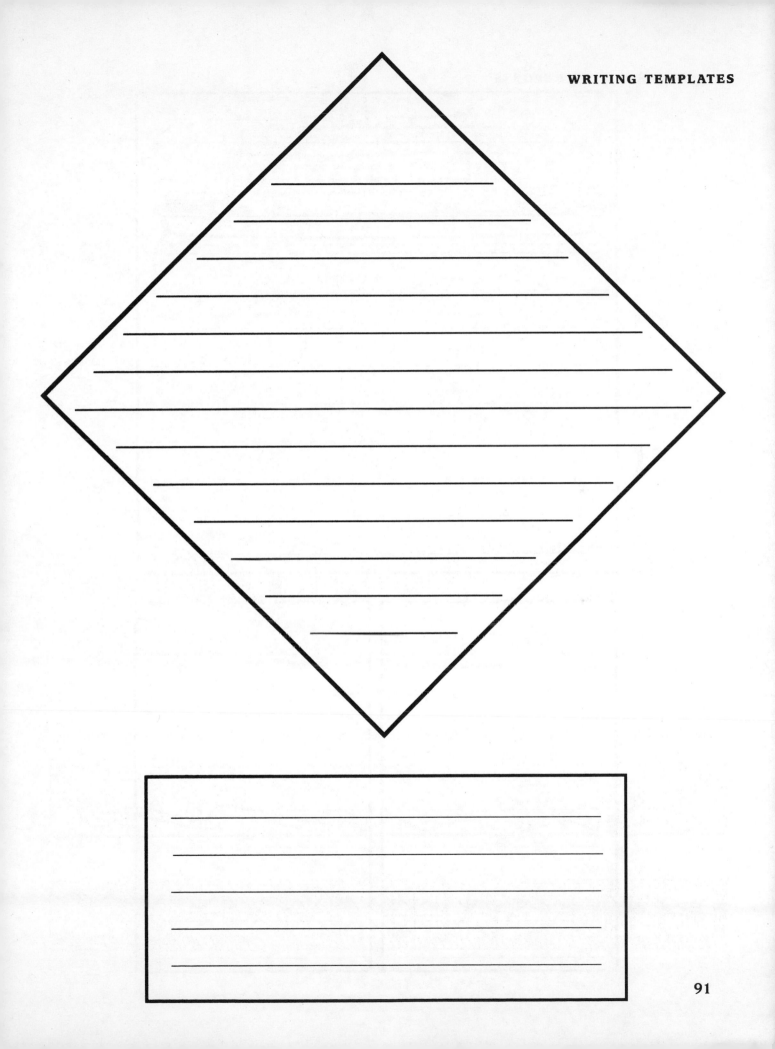

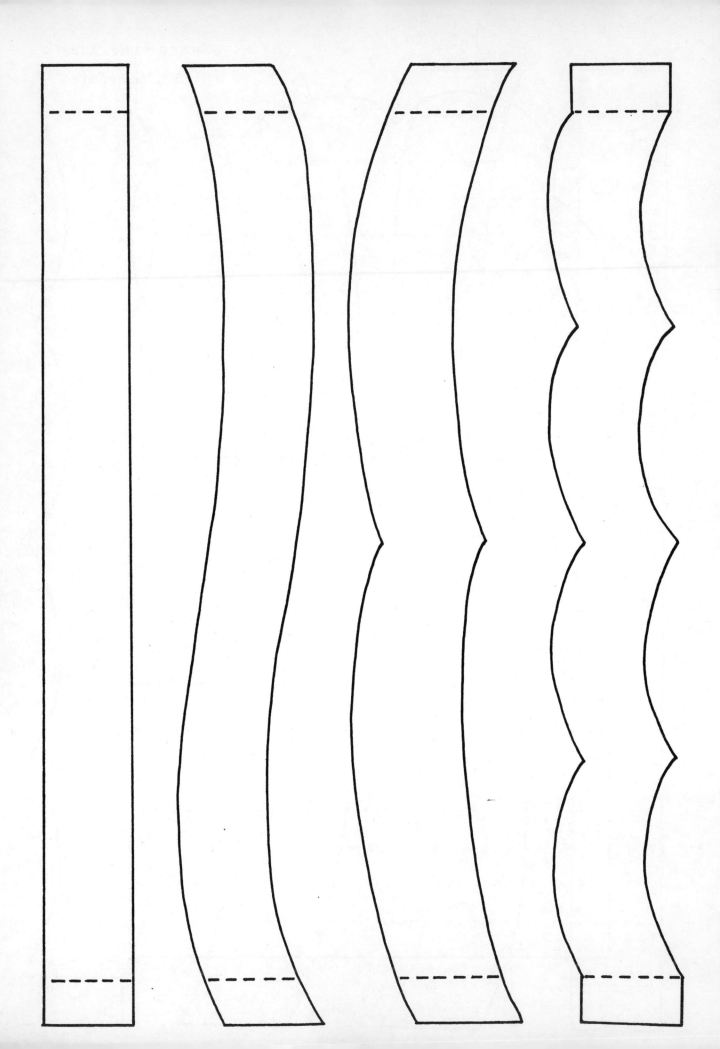

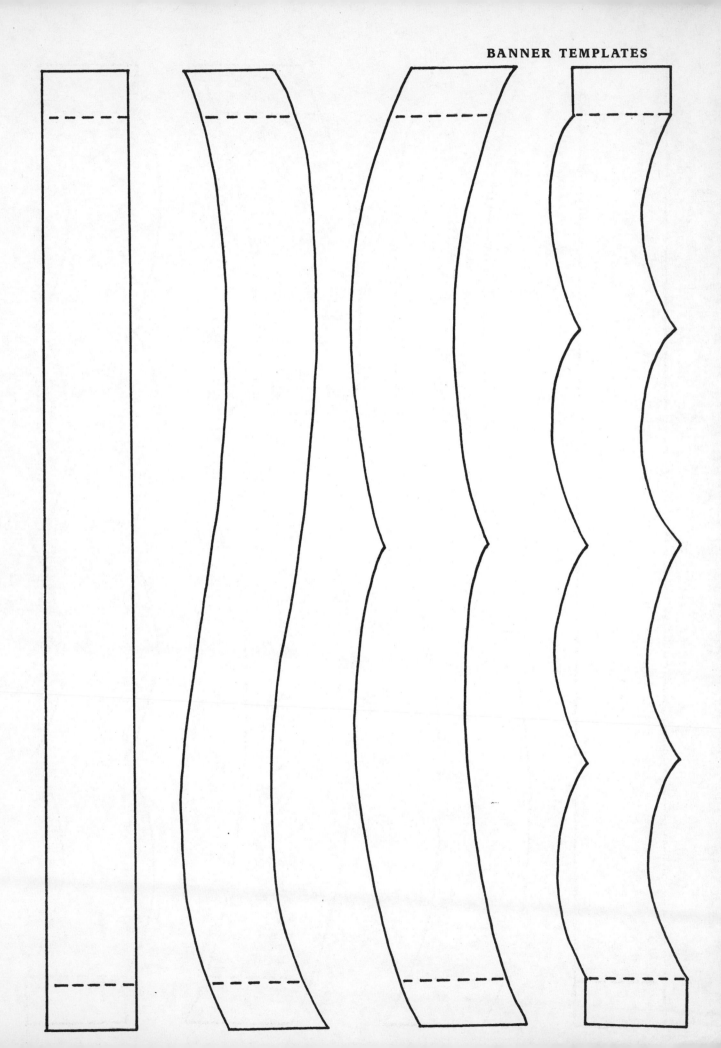